PRAYER BOOK INTERLEAVES

CONCELEBRATION

The ancient manner of celebrating mass at Rome is illustrated in this IX century ivory
panel, preserved at Frankfort-
on-the-Main. The bishop
stands behind the altar facing
the people; assisting presbyters stand about the front of
the altar and recite the consecration prayer with the bishop.
Behind the bishop stand several deacons. Today this custom of concelebration, i.e.
presbyters celebrating mass
with the bishop, only survives
in ordination masses in the
Roman Catholic Church; but
it is a common practice in the
Eastern Churches, where the
primitive tradition of only one
celebration of the liturgy on a
single day in any given church
continues to be the rule.

From *Die Elfenbeinskulpturen aus
der Zeit der karolingischen und säch-
sischen Kaiser, VIII–XI Jahrhundert*
by Adolph Goldschmidt; Berlin:
Bruno Cassirer, 1914; Vol. 1,
Plate LIII.

Prayer Book Interleaves

SOME REFLECTIONS ON HOW THE BOOK OF
COMMON PRAYER MIGHT BE MADE MORE INFLU-
ENTIAL IN OUR ENGLISH-SPEAKING WORLD

BY

WILLIAM PALMER LADD

LATE DEAN OF THE BERKELEY DIVINITY SCHOOL

WIPF & STOCK · Eugene, Oregon

Wipf and Stock Publishers
199 W 8th Ave, Suite 3
Eugene, OR 97401

Prayer Book Interleaves
Some Reflections on How the Book of Common Prayer
Might Be Made More Influential in Our English-Speaking World
By Ladd, William Palmer
ISBN 13: 978-1-5326-6434-2
Publication date 8/3/2018
Previously published by Oxford University Press, 1942

New Edition published in conjunction with
Berkeley Divinity School at Yale

PREFACE

MY INTEREST in the important subject discussed in this little book has been long-standing, as many of my old Berkeley students will testify. But, owing to various time-consuming tasks in connection with my administrative work at the School (of which my friends have been well aware), it has been impossible until recently to give the time to this subject which its very great importance deserves. And it was only three years ago, when the Reverend W.B. Spofford, editor of *The Witness*, requested me to contribute a column every other week to his paper, that I was able to begin writing the little papers here reprinted. I had in mind to write many additional Interleaves, but reasons of health demand that I leave the collection to stand as it is. All the Interleaves as they appeared are here reprinted, although it has been necessary to make some slight alterations and adaptations; unfortunately it has not been possible to avoid much repetition. To this collection I have added a few short papers published elsewhere during this period.

In preparing the Interleaves to appear in book form I am indebted to many helpers—questioners and correspondents who have read them as they appeared, to my efficient and faithful secretary, Elizabeth B. Raftery, to my students, and to my assistant, the Reverend C.K.Myers. Above all I owe a debt of gratitude to my devoted wife, who has helped me to prepare the final manuscript for the press, in which she has had the able assistance of my friend and pupil, the Reverend Massey H. Shepherd. My wife has also prepared the index.

My hope is that the moderate price at which the publishers have been able to issue this little volume will increase the number of readers among that group who have the liturgical destiny of the Church in their hands, i.e. the parish clergy; and that they will seriously consider the facts and ideas here set forth.

W.P.Ladd

Berkeley Divinity School, New Haven
June 1941

My husband left a large number of notes in preparation for Interleaves which he had hoped to write. As he had suggested, these have now been worked over, and some of them have been put together under the heading 'Fragments.'

Grateful acknowledgement for permission to reprint is due to *The Witness*, *The Living Church*, and *The Churchman*, to Messrs. Harcourt, Brace and Company for the quotation from T.S.Eliot, and to Professor C.R.Morey for help in securing the frontispiece. My thanks are also due to many friends of my husband for counsel and assistance, and to Mr.William L. Krause of the Oxford University Press for unfailing patience. To the Reverend Massey H. Shepherd my debt is incalculable.

A.T.Ladd

November 1941

CONTENTS

I. HISTORY

II. THE CHRISTIAN YEAR

III. THE HOLY EUCHARIST

IV. BAPTISM

V. CEREMONIAL

VI. ADAPTATION

VII. UNITY

VIII. MISCELLANY

IX. THE QUESTION BOX

X. APPENDIX

I have known two worlds, I have known two
        worlds of death.
All that you suffer, I have suffered before.
Does the spring change, does the bird's wing
        change, does the fly alter
Its purpose since the amber-time, the old time?
There shall always be the Church and the
        World
And the Heart of Man
Shivering and fluttering between them, choos-
        ing and chosen,
Valiant, ignoble, dark, and full of light
Swinging between Hell Gate and Heaven Gate.
And the Gates of Hell shall not prevail.
Darkness now, then
    Light.

T.S.Eliot, *The Rock.*

I. HISTORY

1. FOURTH-HAND RELIGION

HISTORIC TRADITIONS may be a great asset to a Church. But they may serve, as with the Pharisees in the New Testament, to make the word of God of none effect. Antiquity is a good thing, but not too much of it at any one time. Excessive devotion to the old and familiar may make a Church or a churchman ineffective, and even a bit ridiculous.

St. Jerome, the author of the Latin translation of the Bible which we call the Vulgate, began his labors by translating the Psalms from the Greek Old Testament (the Septuagint) into Latin. Later he learned Hebrew and made another and more correct translation. But congregations preferred the old familiar psalter. It did not matter to them that the new translation was nearer the original. They called Jerome a Judaizer. They wanted the translation of a translation. At the Reformation Miles Coverdale, knowing little Hebrew, translated the Old Testament from Jerome's Vulgate. His version of the Psalms became our Prayer Book Psalter. People became attached to it, and it held its own against all revision. They were satisfied, as we are today, with a translation of a translation of a translation. A few years ago our Prayer Book was issued in Spanish. The General Convention decided that there should be no departure from the official text. So our Spanish converts were given 'The Book of Common Prayer according to the use of the Protestant Episcopal Church in the United States of America' in its entirety, from the Golden Numbers to the Thirty-nine Articles, and included therein was the Psalter, which was thus a translation of a translation of a translation of a translation.

The converts were few, and no great harm was done. But there is always a real and serious danger in a state of mind which cherishes, or which submits to officials and scholars who cherish, fourth-hand expressions of religion. Unfortunately there are not a few parts of our Prayer Book which are products of this state of mind. There are Prayer Book features which have lost their significance but are kept because they are old, once battle-cries, perhaps, in some great theological controversy now extinct. Modification in forms of worship should, it goes without saying, be made with due regard to devotional and intellectual habits. But they should be made. Our Prayer Book is not a Roman missal imposed by an infallible pope, or even an English Prayer Book voted by an omnicompetent parliament, with sanctions and penalties attached.

The only reason for studying past history is that we may learn how to live now. Church history should help us to be better Christians and churchmen. It should clarify and enrich our devotional life. It should be our servant but not our master. It should not chain us to the past, or supply arguments for outworn ideas, or spread content with the *status quo*. It should reveal to us a living God, whose mercies are new every morning, and who has little regard for selfish and stupid habits. It should warn us of that pride which may move us to reject the gospel because we have Abraham to our father, and of that love of this world which when we are not far from the Kingdom causes us to turn away because we have great (historic) possessions.

Liturgical study ought to increase our tolerance and our courage. It will reveal to us that prayer in the first centuries was largely extempore, that before the Reformation services were always changing, and that this living tradition was continued by the English reformers, who declared that 'the Church hath power to decree Rites and Ceremonies.' It ought to give us a sense of great responsibility, because, whether we will or no, for good or for ill, we are ourselves today making history and establishing customs which will outlast our own time and become traditions.

2. OUR HISTORIC PRAYER BOOK

WE HAVE recently been celebrating the 150th anniversary of the adoption of our Book of Common Prayer—a celebration which probably had little interest for most people. In fact many think the Episcopal Church is already far too much concerned with the past. Why spend time, they say, thinking about Bishop Seabury and other great churchmen who are now dead and gone? Does not all Church history, in short, and in fact, belong to the realm of the dead? Let us forget it and apply ourselves to the live issues of our own time.

Others belittle the historical by saying that religion deals with the eternal rather than the temporal, with general principles rather than with particular facts. The Gnostics in the early Church belonged to that class. In their theological system the great role was played by such abstractions as truth, reason, grace, wisdom, and they made light of the historical affirmations of the Apostles' Creed. Similarly the Deists and Unitarians of the XVIII century wanted Christianity reduced to a few essential principles, the religion of all good men. And to this group belong the mystics—for to mystical emotion historical fact can have little meaning.

No one who thinks clearly about these problems of time would deny that the whole past, the distant and the near, the great and the little, is dead and gone for good. It can never come back to us. We cannot go back to it. We live in an ever-new, an ever-different, and an ever-changing world. As Christians we must face the fact that the Christian past, however precious, is non-existent and inalterable. Our duty lies in the present. Now is the day of salvation. No moment but the present is a really sacred one.

But here is the strange paradox—it is only the dead past that can make the present alive! To illustrate, let us suppose that you, reader, should wake up tomorrow morning without a memory. You could not even get out of bed, you would not know the difference between up and down, between the bed and the floor. So with a nation or a Church. It must have a memory. It cannot live, much less progress, except in the light of history. Only as it conserves and forever reinterprets its past does it become competent to act in the present and to deal wisely with live issues and new problems. Christian principles and theological abstractions have their place, of course. But nothing can be less alive than principles and abstractions of any sort. To pin our faith to them is to fall into the scientific fallacy, which is the greatest heresy of our time. Only history can make truth intelligible. Only Christian history can give life to Christian faith.

A disregard of the historic is what often makes the services conducted by our Protestant brethren seem so flat to the churchman. The minister gives the impression of struggling to be contemporaneous. He dwells on general truths which nobody can doubt. If he touches on the historic he does it timidly. Even the ancient prayers which he sometimes uses seem to lack reality.

We do not need then to apologize for Prayer Book anniversaries. It is our duty as churchmen to face modern issues, but equally is it our duty to cherish, to perfect, and to transmit the precious Christian tradition. There can be no divine revelation except by the medium of history. There can be no prevailing prayer except through Jesus Christ and the historic Christian community. There can be no satisfactory common worship except by means of an historic Prayer Book, with its psalms, its creeds, its Bible readings, its holy days, its familiar prayers, and, above all, its liturgy, the great bond between the past and the present.

3. Beginnings of Christian Worship I

In matters of doctrine and liturgy people sometimes choose one particular period of Church history and endow it with special sanctity and authority. The English reformers made their appeal to the first six centuries. The XIII, when scholastic theology flourished, is the favorite century with many. Some exalt the

Reformation age and refer to the writings of Luther and Calvin as if they were Holy Writ. Others, even some Anglicans, insist on building their spiritual home in the Counter-Reformation era, alongside Pope Pius V and the Society of Jesus. And there are those who minimize the past and say we can find God's fullest revelation only in the modern period. Having selected a 'golden age' people are apt to read back into it their own pet ideas. That is a favorite method with Roman Catholic apologists. They find Roman doctrines everywhere. An example is the decree of the Council of Trent, according to which the seven sacraments (a XII century idea) were instituted by our Lord himself.

As a matter of fact it is futile to search for a golden age or an authoritative age. The past has no value except as it is linked with the present. The Church has proclaimed the truth in every century, and being human as well as divine, it has in every century lapsed into grievous error. The student of Church history must try to discover both the beacon lights and the warnings, and should seek to interpret both for the benefit of his own time.

There are, however, certain periods which are especially valuable for our admonition and instruction 'upon whom the ends of the world are come.' Chief of these, to which all Christians look for guidance, is the early period. For the Church was then not only close to the New Testament revelation but it was contending earnestly for its faith in a hostile pagan world—thus it had every reason for preserving the New Testament ideal undefiled. And it is a simple historical fact that in the first three centuries the Church faced all the fundamental problems of doctrine, discipline, and worship, and laid the foundations on which it has been building from that day to this.

Can we recapture the spirit and the way of life and thought of those first days? Perhaps not. But for the realization of Christian unity it is a hopeful fact that all branches of the Christian Church acknowledge the special authority of this primitive period. Strangely enough, the possibility of Christian unity on the basis of the primitive liturgy has as yet hardly been explored, or even considered.

Until a few years ago Justin's celebrated account of the Eucharist in the II century and the chapters in the 'Apostolic Constitutions' giving the Eucharist as celebrated at the end of the IV century were the only important documents known, bearing on the development of the Eucharist in this early period. Now we have three more documents, all of first-rate importance—the '*Didache*' (early II century), the 'Tradition of Hippolytus' (early III century), and the Prayer Book of Serapion, Bishop of Thmuis in Egypt (IV century). The Leonine, Gelasian, and Gregorian Sacramentaries supply valuable data by which to judge the liturgical development of the Western Church in the V and VI centuries. Papyrus fragments, recovered from the sands of Egypt, have made their contribution. And all these liturgical texts may be supplemented by information drawn from many of the Church Fathers, both East and West. Much in the history of the primitive Eucharist remains obscure. Yet we can today reconstruct its history in outline, from its origins in the worship of the synagogue and the New Testament tradition to the developed forms which passed over to the medieval Church and have come down to our various churches in modern times. From this history, so painstakingly and skilfully reconstructed by modern historical research, certain definite liturgical principles come clearly into view.

4. Beginnings of Christian Worship II

THE GROWTH of the Christian Church in the first centuries of its existence is one of the supreme miracles of history. Starting with the little group of disciples of whom we catch glimpses in the four gospels, watching its advent to the chief cities of the Roman Empire as we can observe in the Acts and in the Epistles of St.Paul, its congregations composed of 'not many wise, not many mighty,' we find the Church had spread by the end of the primitive period to the confines of the Mediterranean world and beyond; it had developed a theology and culture which had partly assimilated and partly replaced those of Greece and Rome; and it had perfected an organization which was destined to carry on the administrative and civilizing task of the Roman Empire and to extend it throughout Europe.

The enormous vitality revealed in this first missionary expansion must have had its counterpart in the field of worship. Such unique spiritual experiences do not, however, leave any adequate record, and no amount of historical learning can summon an early Christian Eucharist back to life again. But modern liturgical science does enable us to recognize the presence in that Eucharist of certain fundamental activities or principles, of which four may be briefly summarized.

1. Joy. The very name Eucharist, thanksgiving, embodies this principle. Joy in God's creation, thanksgiving for the fruits of the earth of which bread and wine are the symbols and which the liturgical thanksgiving makes holy. Joy and thanksgiving above all for God's redemption wrought by Jesus Christ, the crucified and risen Lord, in whose triumph over sin and death the Church and the communicant as a member of the Church partakes through faith. 'Let us give thanks.' These were the apostles' words. They belong to the very heart of the service today as at the Last Supper. This abounding spirit of joy and thanksgiving among the apostles made the Church irresistible, for it sprang from the sort of faith that removes mountains and overcomes worlds. And its joy and faith were as far as possible from that artificial enthusiasm which our choirs and congregations often try so hard to inject into our own Prayer Book worship and music.

2. Offering. An integral part of the Eucharist was the offering of bread and wine. Part of the offering was given to the poor. Each communicant was an offerer. He gave his own and he gave himself 'in Christ.' His sacrifice differed from the Jewish and pagan sacrifices in that it was identified symbolically and practically with the

sacrifice of Christ. Bishop Seabury brought the idea of the holy
sacrifice back into our Eucharist, but we have not yet grasped its
full significance. Our worship remains self-centered. We do not
think of the Eucharist as a dedication service, and we seem to
have little success in tying it up with the outgoing Christian life,
e.g. with social service or missions.

3. Unity. Each worshipper shared in the worship of the whole
Catholic Church, earthly and heavenly. Brotherhood and loyalty,
democracy and equality, were spiritual realities having a supernatural basis. The eucharistic fellowship excluded any distinction
between aristocrats and slaves. It was not undermined by snobs
and money-grubbers, our fifth column today.

4. Holiness. To be a communicant meant to be a part of the
Holy Church wherein dwells the Holy Ghost. Only the holy
could offer. The unconverted and even the penitent were excluded
from the holy mysteries. To be a Christian meant to live a disciplined life, to be ready to live and to die for Christ. What a contrast to our easy-going eucharistic worship which demands so
little of us by way of moral achievement!

5. THE LITURGY IN THE MIDDLE AGES I

THE CONTROVERSY over the Middle Ages still goes on. We can
no longer think of them with the naïveté of a Sir Walter Scott or
a Cardinal Gasquet, or a Dean Inge. Certainly the Church has
never in any age produced systematic theologians superior to the
great medieval galaxy—Anselm, Albertus Magnus, Bonaventura,
Thomas Aquinas, and the rest. Medieval scholasticism, rejected
at the Reformation, commands increasing respect today among
theologians of all the churches, and philosophers of all schools. Our
universities came from the Middle Ages. Medieval church architecture is unsurpassed. How good it was may be judged by the
millions we are today spending (and wasting) on copies of Gothic
cathedrals and parish churches. And in other arts the medieval

Church attained the highest levels, e.g. in sculpture, stained glass, and illuminated manuscripts.

As to medieval worship, it was, no doubt, impressive pageantry. And yet the candid student must agree with Father Gregory Dix's judgment that this was 'an age of unexampled liturgical decay,' and that 'underneath all its unessential ornament the heart of the liturgy slowly withered.' To demonstrate that thesis would require a volume, but as such a volume still remains to be written, it may be worth while to attempt a brief summary in this and the next Interleaf of how the medieval Church went astray in this all-important field.

When the Roman empire fell before the barbarian invaders, the Latin language quickly became unintelligible to all except the learned. The clergy naturally, and perhaps inevitably, clung to Latin as the language of worship. It made the Mass into a mystic rite at which the part of the laity was simply to be present and to look on. The clergy turned their backs to the people, built their altars against the east wall of the churches, and hid themselves behind elaborate rood screens. This unnatural separation of clergy from laity was one of the chief causes of the eventual Protestant revolt.

In the primitive period the Lord's Supper was a sacrament of unity, the Christian family meal, the chief community service on each Lord's day, when at one altar (as is still the case in the Eastern Church) all partook of the one loaf. But in the Middle Ages lay communions almost ceased. The monasteries popularized low mass which could be said by the priest alone with no choir or congregation. Altars and masses multiplied for 'each mass as a propitiatory sacrifice had a definite value before God; therefore two masses were worth twice as much as one' (Fortescue). And the more masses the more money for the clergy. The deplorable practice of purchased masses once begun never ceased—and still clings, like the old man of the sea, to the modern Roman Catholic Church. Meanwhile the clergy loaded down the primitive form of the Mass with inferior prayers and with novel ceremonial devices, sometimes of superstitious origin, like the 'last gospel.' And the laity adopted extra-liturgical practices, like the Rosary and the cult of the Sacred Heart, with which they occupied themselves while the miracle of the Mass was taking place at the altar. These devotional novelties led straight on to the sentimental trivialities of the Counter-Reformation period and to modern Protestantism at its worst.

6. The Liturgy in the Middle Ages II

IN THE LITURGY of the primitive Church there were no prayers to Christ; all prayer was directed *to* God the Father, *through* Jesus Christ, *in* the Holy Spirit. Thus the Eucharist had a trinitarian background, as Baptism had, with its creed and its triune baptismal formula. This is still true of our Prayer Book Eucharist, though there are three Reformation collects addressed to our Lord. This primitive tradition was lost in the Middle Ages, and eucharistic worship tended to become Christocentric. At the end of the VII century the *Agnus Dei* was added to the service, and at about the same time sentimental theologians launched the idea that every part of the Mass should be related to some event in our Lord's earthly life, an idea which eventually produced a farrago of childish symbolism, some of which still survives in our devotional manuals. The neglect of the first person of the Trinity led to the abandonment of Old Testament psalms and lessons, and the oblivion of the third person of the Trinity was a natural consequence of the fact that the Roman Mass had no invocation of the Holy Ghost. In the XI century a quarrel over leavened and unleavened bread broke out between the Eastern and Western Churches, and, strange as it may seem, this absurd and disgraceful episode contributed greatly to the Christocentric development. It fixed the attention of the Western Church on bread, on the body of Christ, on the words 'This is my body,' on the advent of the body of Christ to the altar at the moment when the priest uttered the mystic words as the central act of the Mass, the only part that really mattered.* It was an easy transition to the idea of the holy sacrifice as reproducing the death of Christ, and as furnishing security against the pains of purgatory and the flames of hell.

There is still space to touch upon one other aspect of medieval 'liturgical decay.' Primitive Christianity was a religion of sacrifice, but it was also one of joy. The eucharistic service was one of thanksgiving and joy. The disciples were 'filled with joy and with the Holy Ghost' (Acts xiii. 52). This was because their faith was fixed on the risen Lord. Their joy contributed greatly to their victory over paganism. But with the fall of the western empire a difficult time began, a time characterized by invasion, war, hunger, anarchy, frustration, untimely death. General gloom settled upon the world, and the distracted Christian believer turned toward penitence, fasting, humiliation, and asceticism, as the best approach to an avenging deity. This attitude of mind finds expression in many of the medieval collects, e.g. that for the Fourth Sunday in Lent.

In the first centuries the crucifixion had been inseparable from the resurrection, but now crucifixion reflects the mind of the age better than resurrection, and the crucified Jesus supersedes the risen Christ. Constantine had identified the place of the Lord's grave in Jerusalem, and had built over it the church of the *Resurrection*. But in the XI century it has become the church of the *Holy Sepulchre*. Warriors took the cross, set out to capture Jerusalem, and brought back with them a vivid realization of the sufferings of Calvary. The influence of the crusades was far-reaching. In the early period, there had been few crosses or crucifixes, and none upon the altar. But now on every altar appears a crucifix,

* For the details of this remarkable development see Josef Rupert Geiselmann, 'Die Eucharistielehre der Vorscholastik' (*Forschungen zur Christlichen Literatur- und Dogmengeschichte*, Bd. 15), Paderborn, F. Schöningh, 1926, a book which seems to have been surprisingly ignored by English and American writers.

and not in the earlier style which depicted the living, reigning, Christ, but one representing the man of sorrows, crowned with thorns, and dying in agony. This over-emphasis upon the death of Christ passed on into Protestantism. It is reflected in our Prayer Book Eucharist. It is a part of 'the lost radiance of the Christian religion.'

7. LUTHER AND THE MASS

IN THE CENTURY preceding the Reformation there were many enlightened and moderate-minded churchmen who might have brought about a reform of existing liturgical abuses. But the Protestant revolt put an end to any hope of moderate reform. Luther, with all his piety and courage, was a person of violent temper, a believer in strong-arm methods, and a passionate hater as well. Thus the movement he led was protestant, controversial, and negative from the start. Calvin adopted Luther's ideas, and built them into a theological fortress from which his followers could contend earnestly for the new faith. The papal forces, under the lead of the Jesuits, carried on a relentless counter-attack. Of this whole period an English historian, Professor York Powell, has said 'It is a pitiful tale of bigoted ignorance, a long-drawn-out reign of terror.' It was no time for liturgical reform.

But, as in every period of Church history, the good and the bad were mingled. We tend to make the reformers responsible for the low standards of Protestant worship which prevail today. But this liturgical deterioration reflects the pietism and the humanism of the XVIII and XIX centuries rather than the spirit of the earlier Protestantism. Luther was far from being a liturgical iconoclast. His eucharistic doctrine, the so-called 'consubstantiation' theory, exactly reproduced, contrary to the general belief, the Catholic doctrine in which he was reared. 'The High Mass celebrated by the papists is right,' he said. And the Lutheran chorales were surely one of the most sublime contributions ever made to liturgical worship. Of Calvin a contemporary eulogist said, 'His was a character of great majesty.' And in the Calvinistic worship there inhered a majestic element. Nowhere has the Eucharist been more highly regarded than among the Scotch Presbyterians. And both Luther and Calvin wanted it to be the chief act of worship on every Lord's day.

The worst features of Luther's liturgical system came to him from the XV century. Several points may be noted:

1. Individualism was a characteristic development of the late medieval Church. It found expression in mysticism, introspection, sentimentality, and extra-liturgical devotions. Individualism has its merits, but eucharistic worship is essentially corporate. The greatest weakness of modern worship, both Catholic and Protestant, is its exaggerated individualism. Much of the responsibility for this must rest with Luther.

2. The medieval Church fell into sacerdotalism, that is, it set the priest apart from and above the people. Luther called the common people 'swine,' he fought the peasants, he made himself a Protestant pope. And the reformed worship was not something which the pastor did with people, but what the pastor (or the preacher) did for the people. This was the old sacerdotalism in a new but not an improved form.

3. The offering was from primitive times an essential eucharistic feature. But in the late Middle Ages the Mass had become a propitiatory sacrifice which, endlessly repeated, brought vast incomes to the clergy. So Luther threw over the whole idea of eucharistic offering and sacrifice.

4. St.Thomas Aquinas had developed a theory of 'transubstantiation' to refute a carnal conception of the sacramental body of Christ. It was a metaphysical definition and a fit subject for scholastic debate. Unfortunately the problem of the presence became under Luther's influence a battle ground upon which the different sects of Protestants concentrated their efforts and warred against the old Church and among themselves. These metaphysical pre-occupations are, alas, still with us.

8. THE FIRST PRAYER BOOK OF EDWARD VI

TO NO ONE does the Book of Common Prayer owe so much as to Archbishop Thomas Cranmer. Though he was a gentle soul, and inclined to surrender to bloodthirsty people like King Henry VIII and Cardinal Reginald Pole, he was a person of fundamental courage and integrity, as was demonstrated on the day of his tragic martyrdom. He was an Erastian, that is, one who believes the civil ruler has the right to administer the affairs of the Church. But he did not invent that idea. It dates back to the Emperor Constantine in the IV century, it dominated the Frankish Church from Clovis till after Hildebrand, it prevailed widely throughout the whole Middle Ages, it has always been the teaching of the Eastern Orthodox Church. And although Cranmer faithfully served the civil authority under Henry VIII and Edward VI, he had his own ideas about reform. The chief defects of the Prayer Book of 1549, which is largely his work, are not Erastian but medieval. That book was, however, a notable achievement. Its literary pre-eminence is due to Cranmer. And its influence on the religious life and language of England is second only to that of the English Bible. It is the greatest of Prayer Books. It appeared in a polemic time but it was an irenic book. It was wisely planned to satisfy the devotional needs of differing theological parties. It skilfully combined the old and the new. It followed that *via media*, which is the Anglican ideal and one name for any genuine Catholicism. It carried the English Church through the stormy seas of that 'reign of terror,' the Protestant Reformation—yet 'so as by fire.'

For true reform is always difficult, and moderate reform is always attacked by extremists on both sides. The new Prayer Book was quickly drawn into the thick of theological controversy. When the conservative Bishop Gardiner praised it, the Calvinist die-hards (led by a continental divine) attacked it at exactly those points which the bishop had approved. After three years the extreme reformers got the upper hand, and they issued a revised and greatly inferior book, which is substantially the English Prayer Book of today.

But the first Prayer Book of Edward VI could not be destroyed. It remained the ideal to which churchmen turned back again and again. Archbishop Laud in the XVII century was, like Cranmer, a scholar and a man of letters. He inspired the Scottish book of 1637, which in large measure reproduced that of 1549. But Laud's book fell a quick victim to Presbyterian fanaticism and to civil war. Fifty years later came the Non-jurors. They were Anglicans of the Cranmer type. They were as opposed as he to papal obscurantism. They recognized the affinity of the Church of England with the Eastern Churches. They were zealous students of the liturgy. They argued for the symbolic character of the ancient liturgical terminology. They appreciated the significance of the eucharistic offering, and a learned work entitled *Unbloody Sacrifice* was written by one of their number.

Their Eucharist was based on that of Cranmer's first book. Thus it retained the offering and the invocation of the Holy Ghost in its Prayer of Consecration. Happily for us, Seabury was ordained bishop by the Scottish Non-jurors, and accepted their liturgical ideas. It would have been a gain if American churchmen had closely followed the Seabury tradition rather than attempting, as some have done, to copy the Sarum customs of the XV century, or the 'Western use' of the Roman Catholic Counter-Reformation.

9. THE ROMAN MASS

IN THE XV century a demand arose from all over Europe for a reform of the Church 'in head and members.' Reforming councils were held, and if they had been successful they might eventually have achieved a long-overdue revision of the liturgy. But reactionaries in Church and State combined, under the leadership of the papal curia, to stifle all reform. The lid was clamped down, and in the XVI century the great Protestant explosion came.

The Counter-Reformation followed the Reformation. It was a protest against a protest. Its leaders were animated by an uncompromising hatred of reform. They could not act temperately or wisely. The Council of Trent corrected some abuses. But it fought against any change in the Mass. It would not even restore the cup to the laity, though its withdrawal had already lost Bohemia to the Church. In 1570 Pope Pius V made the unreformed medieval rite official. Henceforth this stereotyped form was to take the place of the living liturgy.

The Roman Mass is still that of Pius V. Its defects are obvious. It is in Latin, and is thus a clerical rather than a congregational form of prayer, though much of its Latin is commonplace, and some of it is ungrammatical. It has collected in its long and chequered history, and it still retains, many elements which encumber, obscure, and pervert the primitive liturgical tradition. It is so complicated, especially by reason of its overloaded calendar, that even the celebrating priest needs the help of extra directions prepared by experts. Though it is the Eucharist—the thanksgiving—it hardly strikes the note of thanksgiving. Though it is a sacrament of the Holy Spirit it has no 'invocation' and hardly recognizes the existence of the Holy Spirit. Though it is constantly called the holy sacrifice it belittles the offering and 'does not,' to quote an American Roman Catholic monsignor, 'clearly bring out the doctrine of sacrifice.' Though it has so-called introits, graduals, and communion psalms, they seldom have any reference, as they were meant to do, to the days to which they are assigned, and have in fact lost their original character as psalms. The consecration does not begin, as in the ancient liturgies, with the *Sursum Corda*, but with the so-called Canon, which has been reinterpreted and reprinted to accord with the scholastic doctrine of transubstantiation. The Canon itself, though it was declared by the Council of Trent to be 'free from every error,' contains what a modern Roman Catholic writer describes as 'abrupt transitions, reduplications, and harsh constructions,' and is, according to an

Anglican scholar, 'little better than a medley of incongruous elements.'

How then, it may be asked, does this imperfect service hold its own and continue to attract crowds of worshippers? The answer is simple. The Roman Church (quite rightly) requires that the faithful shall attend Sunday mass. ('If attendance at Sunday mass were not obligatory would ten per cent attend?' asks the above-quoted monsignor.) Since the late Middle Ages the emphasis in Roman theology has been increasingly upon mysticism, that is, religion independent of good conduct, with the result that the Mass has been reduced to an individualistic mystical act of devotion when the bell rings and the priest elevates the host. All this tends to attract many devout souls and has helped to popularize the Mass. This unfortunate development is carried even farther in the Counter-Reformation service of Benediction and the encouragement of communion from the reserved sacrament. Finally, the Mass survives because, with all its defects, it is still 'on the side of the angels,' it retains many primitive and evangelical features, it is the Lord's service on the Lord's day, it continues to 'shew the Lord's death till he come.'

10. JOHN WESLEY AND THE LITURGY

IT WAS SAID of our Lord that the common people heard him gladly. And it ought to be possible to say of our Lord's service, the Holy Eucharist, that the common people gladly hear it and participate in it. It was so in the early Church. But in the Middle Ages the common people could not understand the Latin service, and ceased except rarely to partake of the Lord's table. The recently discovered autobiography of Margery Kempe, written in the XV century, reflects this situation. She applied to the Archbishop of Canterbury to be permitted to communicate weekly. A license 'signed and sealed' was delivered to her, and it 'comforted her soul,' she says, especially as the Archbishop's clerks took account of her poverty and remitted the customary fee. Thus did the medieval clergy build barriers and toll gates around the Lord's table. And yet the mass continued to attract. That was because the clergy changed it into a service at which the only obligation of the faithful was to watch the priest elevate the host. And because in place of the communion meal they were given the 'holy loaf' (as still in the East and in some parts of the West), and on the great festivals unconsecrated wine.

The reformers undertook to revive the primitive Lord's Supper. They abolished the elevation and the holy loaf, and urged frequent communion. But their well-meant efforts failed. The Eucharist under their influence ceased to be the chief act of Sunday worship. Thus was lost the most ancient and precious of Christian traditions, and Protestantism became what Dom Guéranger once called the 'anti-liturgical heresy.'

The Church of England had its Prayer Book, and thus the liturgical way of life was kept alive. But when in the XVIII century, the heyday of the Whig bishops, the easy-going parsons, and the infrequent Eucharists, a prophet arose in the person of John Wesley, the Church knew not the day of its vindication, and literally stoned him. In 1938 many Anglicans, including the Archbishop of Canterbury, joined with Methodists throughout the world in observing the 200th anniversary of Wesley's 'Aldersgate Experience.' That a priest of the Church of England should have had a religious experience was a strange reason for such an elaborate commemoration. And, unfortunately, it identified Wesley with modern Methodist prayer-meetings, whereas he was essentially a Prayer Book churchman, and the embodiment of Anglicanism at its best.

Reared in the churchly atmosphere of his father's vicarage and of Oxford University, he came to an understanding of sacramental theology by a study of the Fathers, of Jeremy Taylor and other Caroline divines, and of non-juring churchmen like William Law. In his preaching tours throughout England he always attended the services of the parish church. He received communion weekly, and indeed as many as four times each week on the average throughout his entire ministry, so it has been estimated. He urged the duty of constant communion. And his communion services attracted the common people beyond the capacity of the churches to hold them. Few priests in any period of Church history have ever done more to popularize the Holy Communion.

His one lapse from Anglican order—laying his hands on Coke— is to be explained in part by his acceptance of St.Jerome's teaching of the equality of bishops and presbyters, but chiefly by his intense conviction of the importance of the Holy Communion. It was a desperate step, but he took it only after he had repeatedly failed to persuade the English bishops to provide bishops and sacraments for his American Methodists. Seabury similarly failed. The two were in London at the same time. If they could have met and agreed on a common plan of action it might have changed the religious destiny of the new world.

11. THE OXFORD MOVEMENT AND LITURGICAL DEVELOPMENT

THE XVIII century was an age of rationalism and skepticism, but in the opening years of the XIX century there was a religious revival all over Europe. Kierkegaard in Denmark, Schleiermacher in Germany, Lamartine in France are names which characterize the new age. It was inevitable that England and the Church of England should share in this general revival. But it was most unfortunate that the leadership should have fallen to such men as Keble, Newman, Pusey, and the others who formed a nucleus at the University of Oxford from which the revival took its name 'The Oxford Movement.' They were sincere, earnest, conscientious, high-minded. But they were typical conservatives and aristocrats. They had none of John Wesley's love for the common people or his willingness to give and take in the world as it is. Keble was a professor of poetry, though of his *Christian Year*

Lord David Cecil in his *Oxford Book of Christian Verse*, says it is 'feeble stuff, a sentimental concoction in ecclesiastical Victorian mock-Gothic.' Newman was a writer of genius, but his obsession with apostolic successions and papal claims led him to think all modern problems could be solved by edging nearer to the pope, into whose unsympathetic lap he finally tumbled. Pusey was a typical Oxford pedant who studied the ancient Fathers to find out what they thought of the prophet Daniel, and published his findings in an absurd English commentary. He issued some polemic tracts against Rome, but balanced them with a series of translations of Roman devotional literature—another 'sentimental concoction.' Their appeal to ancient and medieval precedent was handicapped by their lack of historical knowledge. They abhorred all critical study of the Bible such as was going on in Germany, though it was destined to transform our whole theological outlook. And of course the great revolutionary social and political changes that were taking place all over Europe were quite outside their world.

This is a long introduction to a few words on the influence of the Oxford Movement on liturgical development. That was, sad to say, almost wholly bad. We can best understand it, perhaps, if we recall how this new kind of 'High Churchmen' spent millions of pounds in 'restoring,' and spoiling, fine old English churches and in building new churches after what they thought was the 'correct' Gothic manner. Some of them even came to accept the tear-evoking church ornament and architecture of the continental Counter-Reformation period. So instead of building liturgically upon Cranmer, Laud, the Non-jurors, Wesley, they destroyed and restored trying to make the Anglican Prayer Book and usage conform to their favorite views. They introduced low mass. They made eucharistic worship individual rather than corporate. They brought back to ghastly life all the medieval and Reformation metaphysical wrangles over the manner of the presence. They took as their standard first the Sarum use, then the degenerate, legalistic ritual and ceremonial of the Church of Rome, and tried to force the Prayer Book into that procrustean bed, criticizing the laity and all others who did not agree with them as being provincial and uninformed. Of course all this effort to appease the pope only resulted disastrously, as have English attempts in recent years to appease Hitler. And meanwhile it drove away from the Church hundreds of thousands of the best people of England, those who lived in the midlands and the north, and earnest, evangelical Christians of all denominations—including at last even the Methodists.

But to return to Keble's *Christian Year*. It may not be great poetry, but nevertheless it did a remarkable service in rekindling a love of fast and festival in the Church of England. Neale's translations of medieval hymns were also of great value. Thus Keble and Neale made important contributions to the health and progress of liturgiology. For this we should gratefully remember them.

[*Note:* For further discussion of this subject see *Eucharistic Doctrine of the Oxford Movement: A Critical Survey*, by W.H. MacKean, Putnam, 1933.]

12. THE LITURGICAL MOVEMENT

MARIA LAACH is a small lake lying picturesquely amidst wooded hills not far from Andernach on the Rhine. A Benedictine monastery founded in 1093, with a church which is one of the finest remaining examples of the German romanesque architecture, rises above the lake and takes its name from it. This monastery has in recent years become widely known as the center of the 'liturgical movement' in the Roman Catholic Church.

One day, shortly before the World War, five young laymen appeared at the door of the monastery and asked for some instruction on the Mass which they said they had been attending all their lives without any real understanding of its meaning. In the event they spent Holy Week, 1914, at the monastery, attending the special services of the week and listening to instructions given to them by one of the monks, the learned Dom Ildefons Herwegen. The leader of these young men was Heinrich Brüning, the future Chancellor of the German Reich. They were the first of a group which now numbers 3,000 who come to Maria Laach annually to seek a deeper understanding of the Church's liturgy. That Holy Week was the first 'liturgical week'—an institution which has now been copied in almost every Roman Catholic country in Europe and is beginning to take root in America.

Maria Laach began in January 1919 the publication of a series of booklets entitled *The Praying Church (Ecclesia Orans)*, which had a circulation reaching into the hundred thousands. And in 1921 it issued the first *Year Book of Liturgical Science (Jahrbuch für Liturgiewissenschaft)*, a publication which has become the indispensable guide to all who desire to keep abreast of the latest literature in all languages in the field of liturgiology. The distinguished group of scholars who edit these publications—Abbot Herwegen, Prior Hammenstede (now in this country), Odo Casel, and others—are doing an invaluable service to the whole Church, and it would be a calamity if their great work were forced to discontinue through the opposition of the present German government.

The Brüning incident gives the clue to an understanding of the liturgical movement. Its aim is to encourage the laity to understand and take their part in liturgical worship. From the historical point of view it seeks to return to the standards represented by the Bible, the Missal, and the Breviary; and it criticizes many of the medieval devotional accretions as individualistic, sentimental, and subversive of the true spirit of Catholic worship.

Thus the sacrifice of the Mass, they teach, is not something to be conducted by the priest for the people, but is an offering in which the people take their part not only by communion but by actually bringing their bread and wine to the altar, as was done in the V century at Rome. And if the Eucharist is essentially a common meal it is proper that the priest should stand behind the altar facing the people, as is, in fact, still done in the old Roman basilicas. How shocking such teaching must be to those of our clergy whose idea of being 'correct' is to turn their backs to the people even when reading the gospel!

The handicap under which the liturgical movement labors in the Roman Catholic Church is the Latin language and the general rigidity and inadaptability of the modern mass; and also the size of the church, where millions are wedded to the old ways. But the influence of Maria Laach has been enormous throughout Germany, and has created a solidarity in the German Church which has done much to keep up its courage in these times of persecution.

[*Note:* Description of this movement in further detail is to be found in the Appendix to this volume.]

13. THE LITURGICAL MOVEMENT AND OURSELVES

IT WOULD be a mistake to regard the liturgical movement in the Roman Catholic Church as something novel and original. The effort of its leaders to give the laity a place in liturgical worship, their emphasis upon frequent communion, their criticism of the individualism and superstition of late medieval forms of worship, their appeal to the liturgical usage of the ancient Church, the desire which many of them have that the Mass should be translated into the vernacular of each country—these are precisely the ideals which animated the Anglican liturgical movement of the XVI century and produced our Book of Common Prayer.

Cranmer's purpose was admirable. But he was himself a product of the medieval system, and he could not throw off its influence altogether. His liturgical scholarship was of course inadequate if we compare it with that of the monks of Maria Laach, or indeed with that of any competent student of liturgiology today. And he had to act hastily, under constraint, and amidst the clash of contending theological parties. Thus he made mistakes. His work was only a beginning. But it was a splendid beginning.

The daily monastic services had always been congregational; Cranmer made them popular, so popular, in fact, that his Matins has tended to become our chief act of Sunday worship. Anglo-Catholics often turn up their noses at these services, although a learned Roman Catholic, a disciple of Maria Laach, recently remarked: 'We envy you Anglicans your Morning and Evening Prayer.' It is a pity that Cranmer did not make the Eucharist equally congregational and popular, but, under the spell of the medieval idea that the Mass is something which the priest does alone, he drew up a service which almost ignored the primitive idea of an offering by priest and people acting together. And he had to deal with reactionary laymen like the Devonshire rebels who demanded 'that the priest celebrate mass without communicants, except at Easter'!

The Caroline divines corrected some of Cranmer's mistakes and developed an Anglican tradition. The Non-jurors contributed their learning to that tradition, and John Wesley made a valiant effort to carry it to the common people. The leaders of the XIX century Catholic revival might have built on foundations thus laid. But Newman's defection shook their nerves, and stupid persecutions by English mobs and English judges turned many minds toward Rome as toward a city of refuge.

The clergy had now to become skilful copyists of the Roman Mass, i.e. the degenerate Counter-Reformation Mass, in order to qualify as 'Catholics.' That unfortunate medieval heresy, liturgical dualism—low masses for communicants, high masses for non-communicants—established itself in the Church of England. Clerical trippers to Belgium and Sicily checked up on 'correct ritual.' And the English clergy who did not accept this 'Western use' were regarded as hopelessly antiquated.

It is an encouraging sign of the times that so many of the English clergy (led by Father Hebert) are coming under the influence of the liturgical movement. The day may be nearer than we think when we shall no more have red cassocks and 'last gospels' and other such borrowings from XIX century Romanism. That sort of thing provokes in intelligent Roman Catholics only 'an indulgent smile' (quotation from the Roman Catholic *Commonweal*) and blocks real progress. What we need is more of the Non-jurors' love of learning and of John Wesley's zeal for the realities of religion.

II. THE CHRISTIAN YEAR

14. ADVENT

ADVENT IS a dramatic season. To say that is not to decry it. All great institutions, ideas, and movements must be dramatic if they are to win support. Communism attracts its large following because it dramatically proclaims what it calls a 'world revolution.' The Christian religion, the world's greatest drama, ought to be presented with the best dramatic art we can command. Churches with humdrum services misrepresent the gospel of Christ, and deserve to be empty. We must utilize all the resources of tradition and ceremonial, art and learning, to give the Christian message a dramatic appeal. The Church year is one of the best features of our dramatic equipment, and no season is more dramatic than Advent. It must be presented accordingly.

Variety is a chief means of arousing interest and fixing the attention. The Advent services should come as a sharp contrast to those of the Trinity season. They should express expectancy, as the shop windows do. They should not be penitential, but should reflect some of the joy of the great festival to which Advent looks forward.

And we need not be afraid of a moderate introduction of novelty. Why not adopt the beautiful German custom of hanging a wreath or corona in the church with four candles upon it, one to be lighted on the First Sunday in Advent, two on the Second Sunday, and so forth? It is a most useful teaching device.

The Prayer Book gives us effective help. Cranmer's great Advent collect, repeated daily throughout the season, is full of music and good theology. The Bible collect for the Second Sunday and the ministry collect for the Third Sunday both strike obviously fundamental notes. The story of John the Baptist in the last two gospels adds to the dramatic *mise-en-scène*.

The hymnal also helps. Several of the Advent hymns possess a stirring quality, such as few other hymns have. Pastor Nicolai's 'Wake, awake, for night is flying' is, considering both words and music, perhaps the greatest hymn ever written. Then there is 'O come, O come, Emmanuel,' the Advent antiphons so well versified by our great Anglican hymnologist, John Mason Neale, which, strictly speaking, belongs to the period after December 16, but may well be sung earlier. And 'Thy kingdom come' by an American Unitarian, which Percy Dearmer has called 'one of the noblest hymns in the language.' The John the Baptist hymns should, of course, not be used before the Third Sunday. The Prayer Book hymn, the *Gloria in Excelsis*, may well, according to ancient custom, be omitted throughout the season, kept in reserve for Christmas day, and some other 'proper hymn' sung in its place.

The first Advent is a dramatic story, and nothing could be more dramatic than the second Advent when 'He shall come again,' according to that article of the creed, which, since the publication of Schweitzer's *Quest of the Historical Jesus* in 1907, has taken on a new lease of life. These are great themes for the preacher.

15. ADVENT THOUGHTS

IN THE ANCIENT pagan religions there was always a tendency to localize the divine. God was in sacred places and structures, in stocks and stones. And there is something like this spatial theology in Christianity—a reverence for churches, for shrines, even for images.

But in Christianity, as in Judaism, the emphasis is upon time rather than space. The early Church made the first day of the week into the Lord's day. It transformed the Jewish Passover into the Christian Easter and kept Wednesday and Friday as solemn days of prayer. And on this it built its 'circular year,' as it was called, the Christian year, to give it its modern name, with its round of holy days, and weeks, and seasons. Originally in fact the circular year began at Easter, but in the IV century Christmas and Epiphany gained a place in the calendar, then the Advent season, then the First Sunday in Advent, which became the Church's New Year's day.

Advent turns our thoughts toward Christmas, toward our Lord's first historical coming. But it points as well to the divine manifestation of the Epiphany festival. It speaks of the second coming, and the day of judgment, when time shall be no more, at the end of the world. Thus its message goes beyond time and history. No mere historical event could, as a matter of fact, be a gospel. The past is dead. The future is unborn. Between these two non-existent entities stands the present moment, living, time-less, eternal. There is no other reality in the world. Cranmer's glorious collect strikes the true Advent note—'Give us grace that we may cast away the works of darkness and put upon us the ar-mour of light NOW.'

At Advent the living Christ comes again to the Church. The services of the season should be dramatic and 'different.' Ember days come appropriately in Advent. What clearer indication could there be whether or not the Church is prepared for judgment than the quality of the young men who in any year present themselves for Holy Orders? And how about their training? Is the Church concerned? No. Our theological seminaries could hardly be less in the consciousness of the Church if they were all built on moun-tains in the moon. They seem even to be beyond praying for—to judge by the fact that they are omitted from the Ember prayers, and indeed from the whole Prayer Book.

The Advent gospels may well remind us of the need for a new eucharistic lectionary. The Bishop of Michigan has prepared such a lectionary, and one wonders how many Advents will come and go before the Church acquires sufficient courage to follow some-one like Bishop Page rather than the unknown ecclesiastic who in the VII century made the inept selection of Advent gospels to which we still cling. The great parables of the talents, the wise and foolish virgins, the sheep and the goats, belong here. But 'believe it or not,' they are not among the Advent gospels or anywhere else in the Prayer Book—excepting the last, inserted at the 1928 revision under A Saint's Day.

What a gain, too, it would be (and it would not require great courage) to repair another medieval mistake and introduce an adequate Advent Preface like the one to be found in the Eucharist of the new Scottish Prayer Book—'We thank Thee because thou hast given salvation unto mankind through the coming of thy well-beloved Son in great humility, and by him wilt make all things new when he shall come again in his glorious majesty to judge the world in righteousness.'

16. 'PEACE ON EARTH'

WE CHURCH people have not carried that message very far or very effectively. Why not? Chiefly because we have kept the peace so badly among ourselves. And we have, strangely enough, and sad to say, used the sacrament of love and brotherhood, the Holy Communion, as our favorite weapon of war.

It all happened innocently enough. The little flock of Christ's first disciples, placed in a wicked world, expecting their Master's speedy return, felt they must prepare for the coming Kingdom by keeping themselves free from every taint of sin. One unholy member might contaminate the Holy Church and drive away the Holy Ghost. If that one had tasted the heavenly gift and fallen away (Heb. vi. 4–6) he was *ipso facto* excommunicate, and was not to be given a second chance. This devotion to an ideal standard, this excessive corporate solidarity, this regulation of the common life by inflexible discipline, was overdone but heroic, and it goes far to explain the amazing impact which the Church made upon the pagan world.

But war (and excommunication is a phase of warfare) always carries those who indulge in it far beyond what they contemplate at first. In the year 189 a newly elected Bishop of Rome excommunicated the whole Asia Minor Church because it kept Easter on a different day from that to which he himself and his church were accustomed. In the period of the councils excommunication was the constant recourse of those contending mightily for the faith, and the great Churches of Rome, Constantinople, Antioch, and Alexandria and their bishops constantly fell out of communion with one another. In the XI century the Patriarch of Constantinople and the Pope of Rome, after quarreling over leavened *versus* unleavened bread, excommunicated each other, and thus inaugurated a schism which still divides the Eastern from the Western Church. In the XVI century Pope Leo X excommunicated Luther, and Pope Pius V, Queen Elizabeth. Excommunication persisted in the Church of England, and when John Wesley on January 2, 1743, desired to receive the sacrament in his father's old church in Epworth, where he himself had been baptized and had served as curate, the curate said he was 'not fit,' and turned him away.

The essential character of the New Testament Eucharist is that of a common meal, something which everywhere and always signifies fellowship and friendship. In the Acts the disciples continue in the fellowship of the apostles while they break bread from house to house, and St.Paul writes to the Corinthians, 'We are one bread and one body.' Even if it is not actually the Passover meal, it was from the very earliest times closely connected with it, the Passover meal being the fellowship meal of the whole nation, and our Lord's prayer and discourse as recorded in St.John reiterate the words peace, love, unity. In St.John's Gospel and in the early catacomb frescoes the Eucharist is symbolized by the miracle of feeding the multitude. It was the medieval Church which made the Mass the monopoly of the priest, turned communicants into mere onlookers, and pushed the table against the east wall of the church, often making it a mere appendage to an elaborate reredos. The 'holy loaf' (distributed to all) and the 'kiss of peace' survived, but those last remnants of the primitive fellowship meal were dropped in 1549 in the English Book of Common Prayer.

Is it not high time we gave back to the Holy Communion its rightful character? On Christmas day there will be shepherds and kings and countless other worshippers of every sort kneeling around Christian altars all over the world. If those altars could be centers of fellowship, unity, and love they might usher in a new age of peace and good-will on earth.

Are we afraid lest renewed emphasis on fellowship drag this great sacrament down to the humanistic level? There is no danger. It is the Lord's supper. The altar is his table. We are his guests. The food is the Bread of Heaven. The fellowship is that of Christ's mystical body. Every Eucharist proclaims with angels and arch-angels 'Glory to God in the Highest.'

17. The Christmas Gospel

ONE OF THE most important Church councils ever held was that which met at Constance 1414–18, attended by 29 cardinals, 33 archbishops, 150 bishops, and innumerable doctors, abbots, dukes, knights, and burghers. On the night before Christmas 1414 arrived the King of the Romans, Sigismund, later Emperor. The Christmas midnight mass was celebrated at the cathedral by Pope John XXIII, and Sigismund sang the gospel.

This was the Middle Ages when the clergy were in control of the Church, when to 'go into the Church' meant to become a clergyman, when the clergy built great rood-screens to keep the laity out of the sacred chancel. And yet the ancient tradition had survived that the Church is not the complete monopoly of the clergy, and that the Mass itself is a co-operative act in which, while the chief ecclesiastic officiates at the altar, the chief layman may take the important and dignified part of reading the gospel.

How long is our Church to continue the bad medieval tradition (inherited *via* the Puritans) which assumes that the clergy have all authority and all wisdom, that they are, in fact, the Church, and that the laity have little authority and responsibility therein except to supervise its business affairs and to sit docile in the pews on Sunday?

If we want to recognize the laity as something more than businessmen we might do worse than to begin with the Christmas gospel. Suppose, for example, that in Grace Church, Blankville, on Christmas morning, the senior warden, during the sequence hymn, proceeded to the altar, where he was handed the book, and then came down to the middle of the congregation, with Al Brown, president of the Men's Club, on one side, and Cy Dow, superintendent of the Sunday school, on the other, each holding lighted candles, while somebody else burned a little incense (surely not inappropriate at the Christmas season), and he read 'Unto you is born this day in the city of David a Saviour.' Might not such a ceremony do something to help win respect for the Gospel in Blankville?

But I hear the rector objecting: 'Our people would not stand for so much "ritual." ' As a matter of fact they have something equally ritualistic every Sunday when a group of Blankville's businessmen carry the collection up to the altar in solemn procession while the congregation all stand and the choir bursts into song.

'Too much of a novelty.' But the fact is that such ceremonial reverence of the gospel is very ancient (candles were lighted at the gospel six hundred years before they were put on the altar), it has always been a feature of the Eastern liturgies ('the little entrance'), and it survives in diluted form in our rubric—'all the people standing' while the gospel is read.

'My senior warden can't read well.' In this he is like so many of the clergy. But he would probably do no worse than Sigismund did when he sang the gospel *in Latin* at Constance.

'Contrary to the canons.' Then let one of the clergy read the gospel and the senior warden hold a candle.

18. LENT

THE LEARNED English historian, Professor Bury, a severe critic of the Church, once wrote: 'What induced the ancient world to be converted to Christianity was, above all, I think, the cheerful virtue of the Christian life.' This cheerfulness came from the conviction, held by the first Christians, that Christ, of whose body they were members, had, by his crucifixion and resurrection, become the Victor over death and sin. Good Friday and Easter were a single 'festival'; the Christian New Year began, not as did the pagan on January first, nor, as in the later Church, at Advent, but at Easter; and the period between Easter and Pentecost was, says Tertullian, a time of 'exultation,' the 'great fifty days' when all prayers were to be said standing, as the Council of Nicea later decreed. Lent was the time when converts from paganism were instructed and prepared for baptism, which took place each year on the vigil of Easter, and through which the baptized were, to use St.Paul's words, 'buried with Christ' that they might be raised with him 'to walk in newness of life.'

In the V and the following centuries a great disaster fell upon the Western Church. The barbarians surged across the frontiers of the empire. Conditions arose like those pictured in the Seventy-ninth Psalm when the heathen came into God's inheritance 'and made Jerusalem an heap of stones.' This tragic event is reflected in our Prayer Book. Thus the Easter victory began to fade out of the picture. The fifty days of exultation shrank to a week, and finally to the two days following Easter, as in our Prayer Book. The collect for the Fifth Sunday after Trinity, written probably in the first years of the invasion, prays 'that thy Church may joyfully serve thee in all godly quietness,' but in the collects for Septuagesima, Sexagesima, the Third, Fourth, and Fifth Sundays in Lent, written a century or two later, the recurrent thought is not joy but adversity, punishment, relief, defence. And Lent changed its character to a penitential season. The first day of Lent was given the appropriate penitential name Ash Wednesday. And then the forty days of mourning were found to be too few. The Lombard invasion struck Italy hard, and at the end of the VI century the pope added 'those three Sundays before Lent' which, as our low-brow hymn says, 'will prepare us to repent, that in Lent we may begin, earnestly to mourn for sin.'

But to the modern man this medieval gloom does not make much appeal. Even in the Roman Church, Dr. Easton says, there is 'a radical relaxation of the Lenten rules.' And he adds that the Anglican communion agrees with the Roman that 'the medieval rigor was a mistake.' Can the primitive Christian spirit and tradition be recovered? Perhaps not. But Lent might be made once more a season of real instruction, something as much needed today as in pagan times, and for which there are many resources in books and in study classes. 'Pre-Lent' is certainly a superfluity—violet hangings had best be kept in the closet during that period. As to the great fifty days of Eastertide—they might be recognized at the Eucharist by standing from the *Sursum Corda* to the Prayer of Consecration, a very proper time to stand all the year round; and if congregations are too much wedded to the idea reiterated in so many Church handbooks that prayers can only be said kneeling, then Sunday schools might be instructed to pray standing, as the great Council which gave us the Nicene Creed enjoined.

Finally, it should not be forgotten that to try to spread a 'cheer-up' spirit will not of itself recapture the primitive gospel. In the early Church Easter was the counterpart of Good Friday—joy growing out of repentance and abundant sacrifice—the early Christians understood that. To be glorified with Christ we must be also crucified with him.

19. Cross and Crucifix

Soon after Constantine's great victory at the Milvian Bridge, his mother, Helena, was baptized; and in the year 326, although then nearly eighty years of age, she made a pilgrimage to Jerusalem to see and visit the places which had been made sacred by the birth, resurrection, and ascension of Christ. Constantine had already given orders to build a costly church in Jerusalem over the place of the resurrection, and Helena built churches at Bethlehem over the grotto of the nativity and on the Mount of Olives at the spot pointed out to her as the place of the Lord's ascension.

Pilgrimages became fashionable. And as the pilgrims multiplied so did the sacred places and the sacred relics. Antiquarians and dealers in antiques did a rushing business. The true cross was produced, and its value and fame were enhanced by the claim that it had been found and identified by Helena Augusta herself. Pieces of the sacred wood were sold or given to distinguished visitors, and were deposited in various churches (as in the Church of the Holy Cross in Rome) where today they are sometimes shown to the faithful on Good Friday, or on May 3, the day of the 'Invention of the Cross.'

About forty years after Helena, another distinguished and noble lady, Etheria, a Spanish abbess, came as a pilgrim to the holy places. For the benefit of her nuns at home (and for our benefit) she wrote an account of her travels, in which she tells how on Palm Sunday at Jerusalem the children went from the Mount of Olives to the Resurrection Church, waving palms and singing 'Blessed is he that cometh in the name of the Lord'—the original Palm Sunday procession. And on Good Friday, behind the Resurrection Church, beneath the great jewelled cross which had been recently erected on a mound (our Mount Calvary), just as we see it depicted in the Santa Pudenziana mosaic, she watched the people pressing to kiss a piece of the true cross which the bishop held, encased in a silver gilt casket, in his hands, while the deacons stood by to guard against such an accident as had happened a few years previous when someone had bitten off a piece of the sacred wood and carried it away.

These realistic Holy Week observances spread to the West.

Good Friday separated itself from Easter, and the 'adoration of the cross' became a feature of the Good Friday mass at Rome. The misery of the period of the invasions concentrated thought on the suffering Christ. The sign of the cross in common life acquired magic potency. The influence of the crusades, with their zeal for the Holy Sepulchre, tended in a similar direction. Gradually the crucifix displaced the cross in art and in theology. Two hymns well illustrate the difference between the earlier and the later period. 'The Royal Banners,' written for the reception of a piece of the true cross at Poitiers on November 19, 569, is objective and triumphant; 'O Sacred Head,' from the XIII century, is in its original form so subjective and realistic as to be quite repellent.

The degeneracy of much of this late medieval devotion makes the Puritan prejudice against cross and crucifix intelligible. The two crosses printed in the 1549 Prayer Book (at the invocation in the Prayer of Consecration) disappeared in 1552. And against the sign of the cross in baptism so much opposition developed that in our 1789 Prayer Book a rubric was inserted permitting its omission 'if those who present the infant shall desire it, although the Church knoweth no worthy cause or scruple against the same.' Few English crucifixes survived the Reformation.

20. THE CRUCIFIXION AND RESURRECTION

WE LIVE by symbols. That is because we are all poets in some degree. We are not happy with generalizations and abstractions. We prefer emotion to logic. We count on imagination to carry us through the waste land of the humdrum facts. And we discover, as Aristotle did long ago, that poetry is truer than history. In his autobiography the great Irish poet Yeats tells how he *prayed* that his imagination might be rescued from generalization. 'For ten or twelve years,' he says, 'I suffered continual remorse and only became content when my abstractions had composed themselves into picture and dramatization.'

Symbolism does not take us away from reality and truth. There are many kinds of symbols, including the scientific and mathematical. Most important of all are the religious, whereby in the forms of sculpture, architecture, painting, poetry, prophecy, sacraments, and, not least, in such great music as the Bach chorale, we seek and find the divine revelation. Preachers and theologians cannot dispense with symbolic language. A correspondent objects to my linking church services with the theatre, but, as a matter of fact, there is no higher expression of religious faith than is to be found in the dramatic symbolism of the Eucharist. It embodies the Christian gospel not in mere words, like a sermon, or in motionless forms, like a mosaic, but like a drama in significant act. We do not simply listen to the story of the cross, or look at a picture of it. In the bread and wine broken, poured, and offered, we face the reality of Christ crucified. And we accept or reject.

The crucifixion and resurrection live again in the pages of the gospels, but only because they belong to the continuing, visible Church. Good Friday and Easter are not mere commemorations of historic events. They are a part of our corporate Christian life. And it is because of their significance for that life that they are not dead but alive. They do, in fact, express and symbolize the deepest truths of our religion—suffering and death as the prelude to life, and God's triumph over man's sin. St.John expresses this in the words, 'God so loved the world'; and St.Paul, 'God was in Christ reconciling the world unto himself.'

That the early Church subordinated the historic detail of our Lord's death to its symbolic value as the central act in the great drama of redemption is shown by the fact that it did not even observe the anniversary of the crucifixion. It combined what we call Good Friday with Easter. And it transferred both from the actual Passover date to the following Saturday night, the great Easter vigil, when the Lenten fast abruptly terminated, the waiting catechumens were baptized and confirmed, the paschal candle was lit, the Eucharist was celebrated at cockcrow, and the faithful looked for the second coming of Christ.

But, my critical correspondent will say, is not the Holy Eucharist something immeasurably greater than a dramatic representation or a mere symbol? Certainly. It is what the older theologians call *signum efficax*, an efficacious symbol. Sacraments effect what they symbolize. In our Easter Communion we are *really risen with* Christ. In the bread given and received Christ really comes to us, and we *really unite ourselves* with him. The Holy Spirit by these outward forms really enters the hearts of the faithful, and really enables us to die daily from sin and to live daily in the joy of Christ's resurrection.

21. The Easter Communion

PEOPLE SOMETIMES ask—Why bother about the Prayer Book when we are faced with a world at war? It is a fair question, but it provokes another. What shall the Christian bother about? What is the Christian way to face a world at war, and to exorcise the deep-seated inhumanity (of which war is only a symptom) which permeates our own peaceful U.S.A. as well as the warring nations of Asia and Europe? The New Testament has an answer to that question. And St.Paul, if he were here today, would doubtless say to the Germans and Russians, the Japanese and Chinese, the French, English, and Americans, just what he once said to the Jews and Greeks—that Christ crucified and risen again is 'the power of God unto salvation,' and our only hope.

We Episcopalians, of course, agree with that. We are strong for the apostles. We would hesitate to disagree with them on anything, least of all with St.Paul, our special favorite. The Greeks thought the crucifixion foolishness, but we do not. Is it not in the Bible, in the Creed, not least in the Prayer Book, in the very heart of the Holy Eucharist—'his blessed passion and precious death'? Do we not put the cross on our altars, even wear it as an ornament? Sacrificial love is a part of our *Weltanschauung*, our way to deal with a world at war. The Church has the answer.

But wait! Admitting that we do have the right theory about the cross, it may still be asked if theoretical knowledge apart from practice has any value whatsoever. The Bible itself raises that question. Even the devils believe, it says. That statement seems to indicate that theoretical knowledge is worse than valueless, that it has a diabolical character. Perhaps our theoretical esteem for the cross is only an open gate on the road to hell.

The proposition that a purely theoretical knowledge is dangerous finds some support in the present condition of the world. Modern man has for a long time been trying to live on theoretical knowledge, on a strictly intellectual attitude toward human life, on what St.Paul calls 'the wisdom of this world.' Science deals not with stars and atoms only, but with man and his destiny. His creeds are worked out in laboratories. His spiritual directors are the university professors. And we are all so much under the spell of scientific infallibility that the modern mother hardly dares to kiss her baby until she can get the approval of some neighboring psychologist. Now war has descended upon us. The professors of course know all about war. They can describe it from the point of view of chemistry, physics, psychology, economics, and sociology, and they can tell how to carry it on most effectively. It would be unfair perhaps to say that they are responsible for it, but the fact that Germany has the most professors would almost seem to indicate that the more professors there are the more numerous and the more brutal the wars.

St.Paul knew the dangers of the theoretical. To him the supreme reality was the cross, not as an idea only. He bore the marks of the Lord Jesus in his body. The same is true of all great Christians—martyrs, monks, missionaries, in every century, and of the heroic German, Polish, Russian Christians of our own day. Love which shrinks not from suffering and death is the identification tag of the true Christian. It unites him with the crucified, and infuses his life with the power of God.

This brings us back to the Prayer Book. For the Holy Communion, whether at Easter or at any other time, is not a theoretical or scientific affair. Rather it is the irrational, inexplicable approach of God to man. It is not a piece of ineffective mysticism, or an aesthetic thrill produced by lovely music and expensive flowers. It is a great practical reality. It is the manifestation of God's love in Christ, to which the response of the worshipping congregation is: 'We here offer ourselves, our souls and bodies, to be a reasonable, holy, and living sacrifice.' If on Easter day the whole Christian Church were to enter into the fullness of that sacramental experience, it could quickly abolish war.

22. WHITSUNDAY

WHITSUNDAY (i.e. White Sunday) is the Christianized feast of Pentecost, the climax of the great fifty resurrection days. It has been observed in the Church from the beginning. Thus it shares with Easter the distinction of being the oldest Christian festival. And it commemorates one of the greatest events recorded in the pages of the New Testament.

But like the other great days of the Christian year we do not observe it for its historic importance or as a mere anniversary. It belongs to the present. It presents a live issue. The Church today as at the beginning confronts an indifferent and hostile world. It needs a new outpouring of the Spirit. And the Spirit will come, so Whitsunday reminds us, to those who are of 'one accord,' and, to those who are prepared to proclaim Christ crucified not in word only but in act, those who for their faith are ready, like the first disciples, to give up all, even life itself.

Our Lord likens the Holy Spirit to the wind whose movements are unpredictable. On the other hand, he says, the Spirit works through the Church. Let us not forget this. Law and order are superior to anarchy and accident, the community is greater than the individual. Divine revelation and grace work through the sacraments. We are accustomed to connect the Holy Ghost with confirmation. But that should not blind us to the fact that the

Holy Eucharist is essentially a sacrament of the Holy Ghost. So the early Church understood it. The older liturgies not only invoke the Holy Ghost on the elements, they assume that the communicant will receive the virtue of the sacrament through the Holy Ghost. Thus the primitive Eucharist was 'Spirit-centered.'

Sometime after the year 500 all reference to the Holy Ghost (except in doxologies) dropped out of the Roman Mass. This unfortunate event had important consequences. A new eucharistic 'ideology' began to develop. The controversy between East and West over the use of unleavened bread in the Eucharist produced a concentration of interest on the body (rather than the blood) of Christ. Thus grew up an exaggerated emphasis on the words '*Hoc est corpus meum*,' communion in one kind, 'elevation,' transubstantiation, a 'Christocentric' service. The primitive idea of the communicant sharing in the eucharistic offering and being sanctified by the Holy Ghost fell into the background.

This bit of history demonstrates how much we owe to our first American bishop. 'The efficacy of baptism, of confirmation, or orders,' he wrote, 'is ascribed to the Holy Ghost, and his energy is implored for that purpose; and why he should not be invoked in the consecration of the Eucharist, especially as all the old liturgies are full to the point, I cannot conceive. . . [The invocation] would restore the Holy Eucharist to its ancient dignity and efficacy.' Providentially Bishop White, to whom Bishop Seabury wrote this letter (June 29, 1789) agreed, and thus our first American Prayer Book appeared with an invocation in the Prayer of Consecration. Our debt to Bishop Seabury is incalculable, and though he have no place in any calendar we must remember him with gratitude, and at no time more appropriately than on Whitsunday.

We may well recall, too, that Pentecost was the Jewish commemoration of the gift of the Law on Sinai. It may be that the Ten Commandments are out of place in the Eucharist; but this day if ever they should certainly be read.

23. Prayer in the Fifth Century and the Twentieth

It would be a gain if the clergy preached oftener on the collects. First, it would be a novelty, and some novelty is always necessary if congregations are to be kept awake. Second, in preaching and teaching it is always a good plan to start from the familiar. Third, even the most familiar collects do not mean much to the average congregation who need to be taught to pray, not mechanically and by force of habit, but with the understanding. And fourth, sermons on the collects can teach Church history, a vital and challenging subject of which most laymen know little or nothing, and can enforce the Church year.

Take, for example, the collect for the Fifth Sunday after Trinity. That little prayer was written in the V century, in a period of revolutionary change which has many points of resemblance to our own time. The old Roman civilization was going to pieces, though many could not believe it. In the year 405 the emperor Honorius built a triumphal arch in Rome on which was an inscription saying the Goths were 'forever extinguished,' and in another inscription on the wall he built around Rome he called it the 'eternal city.' Only five years later the city fell before Alaric's Goths. In the year 420 the Christian historian Orosius saw the empire breaking up—he was, in fact, driven from his home in Spain by the invaders—but he thought so much affliction would convert the Romans to Christianity, the good old times would come back again, and then everything would go on better than before. The world, however, went from bad to worse. Christians lost their property and their lives. Everywhere confusion, insecurity, fear, disillusionment, despair prevailed.

So the Church prayed that 'the course of this world might be peaceably ordered' by God's governance. We know that that old Roman and barbarian world of the V century never got to the point where it was peaceably ordered. We know that our world is not peaceably ordered, we do not see any immediate prospect of its being peaceably ordered, and we do not seem to be able to do much about it. That is because at the root of the world's disorder is original sin. But the Church continues to pray in faith, praying the same prayer in the V century and the XX, believing that world peace is not an impossibility.

In the collect we also pray for the Church. It is a significant sign of the times that the great English critic and one-time agnostic, Middleton Murry, should have reached the conclusion in a book just published in England, entitled *Heaven—and Earth* that the only hope of preventing this Christian civilization of ours from collapsing into sheer barbarism is in the refounding of a Catholic Christendom. Perhaps our slack and disunited Christendom needs praying for more than the world.

In the collect we pray that the Church may 'joyfully serve' God. Meanwhile we are the Church. By God's grace we can answer our own prayer. 'Joyfully serve'—what does it mean? Certainly not simply singing hymns, or living in happy-go-lucky irresponsibility, least of all being self-satisfied or congratulating ourselves that our own life flows on peacefully and happily. Christian joy is inseparable from penitence, a clear conviction of Christian truth, a constant choice of the eternal in preference to the temporal, self-sacrificing devotion to those things in the community and in our own lives which are clearly in accordance with the will of God. If the Church prayed in such a spirit there might well be peace in our time.

24. ST.JOHN BEFORE THE LATIN GATE

IT IS a pleasant occupation to criticize other people. And it may be a profitable one as well, for if we have sufficient humility we can turn the criticism of others into criticism of ourselves. Let us then, in all humility, take a little fling at the 'Proposed Book' in use today in many parishes in the Church of England, which the preface tells us is the Prayer Book of 1662, with additions and deviations, approved in 1928 by large majorities in the Convocations of Canterbury and York, in the Church Assembly, and in the House of Lords, but voted down in the House of Commons.

We open the book at page 736, and there we find a provision for 'Lesser Feasts,' the first of which is 'St.John before the Latin Gate.' What does this mean? Let us with such fragmentary data as survive try to reconstruct the historical situation. The place is Rome, and the time between 450 and 550, let us say the year 496 when Gelasius was the Roman Bishop. There was a slum section of the city inside the Latin Gate where it was generally agreed there ought to be a church. Money was collected, a dignified church in a somewhat oriental style (ancestor of the church still standing) was built, and in due time the priest in charge went up to the Bishop's office at the Lateran palace to consult him about the dedication of the church. Gelasius was a busy man, fighting heretics, carrying on a voluminous correspondence, writing and rearranging prayers, some of which undoubtedly survive in the famous *Gelasian Sacramentary* and in our own Prayer Book. So he sent his secretary out to talk with the priest; the dedication (under the patronage of St.John) was fixed for May 6, and the day duly entered upon the episcopal engagement pad. The dedication took place. And that dedication day became not only the annual parish festival, but a day on which all the churches in Rome prayed at their altars annually for the little church inside the Latin Gate, and sent their collections to the priest in charge.

And not only in Rome, for when the Roman missionaries came to England they taught the English that it was the correct thing to observe all the days in the Roman calendar, which the English, good children as always of the pope, proceeded to do, and kept on doing until Cranmer in 1549 swept '*Joannis ante portam Latinam*' completely away, along with Adam's birthday on March 23 and many other holy days and commemorations which had cluttered up the medieval calendar. May 6 must have meant a great deal to devout Churchmen in Rome in the VI century, but Cranmer did not see that it had any particular significance for England in the XVI century.

Today the English people are no longer the obedient children of the pope, and many of them are not particularly interested in Church calendars or in the Book of Common Prayer. Indeed, far too many, along with the rest of the modern world, have lost interest in religion altogether. The sudden eruption of paganism and barbarism in the World War and since has brought the Church face to face with the question whether England, America, and the modern world will ever again listen to the gospel of Jesus Christ.

One might have hoped some light would come from the assembled archbishops, bishops, deans, archdeacons, and other clergy who composed the Convocations of Canterbury and York, the distinguished laymen of the Church Assembly, and the whole English aristocracy in the House of Lords. Their proposal to revive the minor festival of 'St.John before the Latin Gate' does not seem to lead the Church and people of England on to firmer ground in this day of disaster.

25. PRECIOUS BLOOD

JULY FIRST is the 'Festival of the Most Precious Blood' in the Roman Catholic Church, a 'double of the first class,' added to the calendar in 1849 by Pope Pius IX. Some of our clergy, with a view to popularizing this festival in our Church, will be printing it this year in their parish weeklies. But before 'we first endure, then pity, then embrace' this Roman intruder, it might be well to consider it against the background of its historical origin of which the following paragraphs are a brief summary.

The cult of the 'precious blood' arose in the period of the crusades. Gullibles returning from the Holy Land had brought back what they claimed were drops of our Lord's blood shed on Calvary. These relics were deposited in favored churches and attracted crowds of worshippers. It was a cult which satisfied the mawkish sentimentality and the preoccupation with death which was so marked a feature of the late medieval Church. And there was another source of the 'precious blood.' Realistic views of the bodily eucharistic presence had become general, and in various churches all over Europe (except in England and Scandinavia) the host or the wine turned red at the mass and became the physical 'precious blood.' Pilgrims to the churches where these relics were shown acquired indulgences and belssings for which they paid vast sums. It was an abuse against which 'reformers before the reformation,' like the Cardinal Archbishop Nicholas of Kues, vigorously protested. But it was never suppressed.

Pius IX became pope in 1847. When elected he was supposed to have liberal leanings, but as pope he was forced to choose between a free, united Italy and Austrian domination. When he chose the latter he found Rome too hot for him; he fled to Gaeta, and sent out an appeal to the Catholic powers. Louis Napoleon came to the rescue, seized Rome, and restored the pope. For the next twenty years, with the aid of French soldiers, Pius ruled the papal states by dictator methods—suppression of free speech, espionage, assassination, and every kind of reactionary policy—until Victor Emmanuel, having overcome the Austrians and the French, annexed the papal domain and occupied Rome in 1870, just as Pius was proclaiming himself infallible. At Gaeta his companion, the Superior of the 'Congregation of the Most Precious Blood,' had suggested to the pope that if God gave him back his papal domain he should in gratitude add the 'Festival of the Most Precious Blood' to the calendar of the Church. The day on which the French took Rome was June 30. Pius chose the next day for the festival.

One wonders what may be the motive of those of our clergy who are cultivating this piece of Romanism. Are they trying to spread political fascism of the Pius IX type? One hesitates to believe that. Is it that the word 'blood' is in our day an effective aid to devotion? The very opposite would seem to be the case. Is it a love of copying? Perhaps. Is it a desire to conciliate the papal dictatorship with a view to eventual union? Mr.Chamberlain tried that policy at Munich, but it did not prove very successful. Is it to promote a 'Western use'? That would seem to mean swallowing every new papal decree, however indigestible.

Many intelligent Roman Catholics must regret the presence of this festival in their calendar. Some in our Church must look on its appearance in parish calendars as an insult to their intelligence. Certainly the clergy who print these calendars (unlike the Heavenly Father—St.John iv.23) are not seeking worshippers who worship in spirit and in truth.

26. ST.AUGUSTINE

IT SEEMS silly to keep the day that Gelasius's secretary may have picked out for the dedication of St.John before the Latin Gate in Rome as a minor festival in the English Church, but how about some of our own major festivals? We observe St.Philip and St. James on May 1 for exactly the same reason—because a church in Rome, perhaps the union of two parishes, was dedicated on that day. And we keep August 24 in honor of St.Bartholomew, although Bartholomew is nothing but a name. There is, of course, an historical explanation of these commemorations. Someone once held the idea that every name in the New Testament must be that of a saint, so he canonized Caesar Augustus and Pontius Pilate; and something of this same idea was in the mind of Cranmer, Calvin, and the other Protestant reformers. The name of an apostle was sacrosanct even if nothing was known of the man to whom it belonged. We do know something of St.John, and a little of the church inside the Latin Gate, but of St.Bartholomew we know nothing at all except that his name appears among those of the apostles.

We cannot think that God abandoned the Church after the last syllable of the New Testament was written, and gave it no more saints. As the medieval Church did, we believe that there are saints in every age, and we would undoubtedly like to commemorate them as the medieval Church did. But in the Anglican Communion we are usually too timid or too lacking in imagination to go beyond what the Prayer Book expressly prescribes. Perhaps we are waiting for some enlightened Cranmer to come along and repair the first Cranmer's mistakes; but if so we may have to wait another four hundred years.

If we want to make a beginning we could not do better than to start on the Sunday next to August 28, St.Augustine's day, a festival that Cranmer abolished, which commemorates the death of one of the greatest of saints, Augustine, Bishop of Hippo, on August 28, in the year 430. No saint of the Church has ever exercised a more beneficent influence than St.Augustine; his influence towered over the whole Middle Ages in the theological, the practical, and the mystical spheres; at the Reformation he was the hero of both Protestants and Catholics. He was a great philosopher, theologian, writer, psychologist, one of the most modern of the ancients, and a man of the most saintly life. We have a great deal to learn from him today.

Two of his books are among the world's masterpieces. The *Confessions* gives an account of his conversion and religious development. The *City of God*, written in the face of the downfall of the Roman empire, forecasts the medieval empire and papacy, and shows how though the earthly city fails there is still a city of God eternal in the heavens of which the Catholic Church on earth is a shadow and a promise. In these days, when civilizations and traditional institutions are crumbling, we can find much by way of instruction and inspiration in this notable book.

The clergy have a great opportunity on August 28 to bring the life and theology of Augustine before their congregations. They do not even need to prepare a lecture or sermon; they have only to read extracts from the *Confessions*. Nothing could be more edifying. Romans xiii, the passage which converted Augustine, could well serve for an epistle or second lesson. On the Sunday, following the saint's day, passages might be read from the *City of God*.

Why not keep a real saint's day instead of one which has no meaning?

III. THE HOLY EUCHARIST

27. THE CENTRALITY OF THE EUCHARIST

HALF THE people of the United States do not belong to any church and of those who do it is safe to say that at least a half do not take their religion any too seriously. All over the country, in every parish, the clergy face the same situation—a few devout supporters, others lukewarm, a multitude indifferent or perhaps hostile. In such a situation what should be the strategy of the Church? Obviously it should concentrate on essentials. That is what the Church did at the beginning—it faced a hostile world, but it knew its own mind, it made itself understood by the plain man, it did not scatter its energies, and it hammered away with its gospel until paganism surrendered. I suggest that the essential on which we should concentrate today is the Holy Eucharist.

'But,' it may be objected, 'would not that be a too narrow policy? Would it not sacrifice many other things which we hold dear?' No, because the Eucharist can be related to every essential element of the Christian faith. It combines doctrine and practice, and we can concentrate upon it without sacrificing anything. Let us see how this works out in detail.

1. Corporate worship—that is what the Eucharist is. And that is the right starting point, the right foundation for the Christian structure.

2. Individual prayer—almost a lost art today and difficult for many people. Our Prayer Book gives a large place (too large in fact) to individual edification. But individual worship is stimulated and directed by eucharistic worship. In the Eucharist we unite our prayers with those of the whole body of the faithful. The

catechism requires faith, love, and repentance from the individual communicant. As expressions of personal religion nothing could surpass some of our eucharistic hymns, e.g. 'When I survey the wondrous cross.'

3. The Eucharist always draws the mind of the communicant back to Christ. It is his sacrament. In the epistles and gospels he speaks. The creed teaches his incarnation. The Christian year dramatizes his life and teaching.

4. All the great Christian doctrines are, in fact, in the Eucharist —yet not as scholastic propositions or authoritarian decrees, but in dramatic form and clothed with life.

5. Not only doctrinal but ethical teaching, as in the 'summary of the law' and throughout our service.

6. And human welfare. The Eucharist proclaims the sanctification of all life. On the altar we offer God's creatures, the bread and wine. And they are not only God's, they are the products of man's labor. No eucharistically minded Christian can possibly say his whole duty is to save his soul and other people's souls. He must be concerned about the body, about hunger and poverty, about unsanitary tenements, ugly cities, and every social injustice.

7. The Eucharist is the Christian family meal. The parish communion unites the parish. From there we proceed toward Christian unity and world unity. And at the Eucharist we commemorate the dead.

8. It is a missionary sacrament. But our Prayer Book does not bring this out so clearly as it might.

Which brings me to a very important conclusion—if we want to give this strategic and manifold effectiveness to the Eucharist, we must perfect our present Prayer Book service. It can and should be made more catholic and primitive, and at the same time more modern and practical, and above all shorter.

One final caution to the clergy: don't bore people by excessive talking about the Eucharist. Take it for granted.

28. THE HOLY COMMUNION IN OUTLINE

OUR PRAYER BOOK Communion service is the product of a long historical evolution. It has been repeatedly revised and reformulated. It has lost much of its primitive simplicity. And the result is that many find it a hard service to understand. But if we are to worship intelligently we will want to grasp the significance of its various parts so far as possible, and not to miss the wood for the trees. Perhaps the following outline will help.

The service has four parts which give expression to four fundamental themes: Revelation (pp. 67–71), Creation (pp. 72–74), Redemption (pp. 76–82), Sanctification (pp. 75, 76, 82–84).

I. Revelation. This is threefold: (a) The Bible, which contains all things necessary to salvation. Selections from epistles and gospels enforce the teachings of the Christian year. On special days, as Ash Wednesday, the Old Testament is read, a valuable reminder of the important place which the Old Testament once held in the primitive Eucharist. (b) The creed, a symbol of revelation through the Church. It reminds us that Christian tradition, equally with Holy Scripture, transmits the knowledge of divine things. It proclaims the fact that God is revealed in history, and that our understanding of Christian truth can grow and deepen. It both summarizes and supplements the Bible. There was a creed before there was a New Testament, but our creed is the statement of a developed faith. (c) The sermon, which applies Bible and creed to our life today. For divine revelation is not something enshrined in the dead past, it is a present living reality.

II. Creation. God manifests his almighty power in the whole world of nature and of man. By thankfully offering bread and wine upon the altar we acknowledge his bounty in nature. And we offer our alms to spread the knowledge of him to our fellow men throughout the world. In the Prayer for the Church we pray not only for the Church, we 'give thanks for all men' and we pray for 'all who are in need,' i.e. for all mankind.

III. Redemption. The *Sursum Corda*, 'Lift up your hearts,' 'We lift them up,' inaugurates, as it has from the earliest times, the central eucharistic act. 'Let us give thanks'—the very prayer used by the apostles themselves. 'It is meet and right,' say all the people. Thus we thank God for the gift of his Son who inaugurated the Lord's Supper, by which his blessed passion and precious death, his mighty resurrection and all the blessings of his redemption become real to us.

IV. Sanctification. This is our part—to become holy by the power of Christ and of the Holy Spirit. We confess our sins, and if in this confession we identify ourselves with the whole Church and the whole of humanity we cannot but say—'the burden of them is intolerable.' Then we offer ourselves to be a 'reasonable, holy, and living sacrifice,' and in our communion we are incorporated anew into Christ's mystical body. Finally, after thanking God for his favor and goodness thus manifested toward us, and praying that by his grace we may carry this 'holy fellowship' back into our everyday lives and 'do all such good works' as he has 'prepared for us to walk in,' we depart in his peace.

29. THE FIRST SUNDAY IN THE MONTH

CHARITY BEGINS at home. And if we are to make the Holy Communion once more the 'bond of charity' (as St.Augustine calls it), and the 'sacrament of unity,' we must begin with our own home parish. Through parish unity we shall move towards Church unity and world unity.

The ideal is that every parish should unite around the Lord's table on every Lord's day. We have seen that such was the custom in the primitive Church. But today we cannot reach that point at a bound. And, in fact, that ideal practice did not last long even in the primitive Church. Already at the end of the IV century St.Chrysostom complains that his congregation in Constantinople left church before the mysteries began. In the VI century St.Caesarius, Bishop of Arles, in order to keep people at the service had to lock the church door, it is said. The Lateran Council in the XIII century ruled that every communicant must receive communion once a year, but according to a chronicler of the next century 'few' observed even this rule. Benedictine monks were supposed to receive on every first Sunday of the month, but repeated papal admonitions indicate that they did not do so. The rule in several religious orders was three times a year. The ordinary worshipper in the centuries immediately preceding the Reformation was satisfied if he saw the priest elevate the host at the Sunday mass, and we are told by contemporaries that many stood outside the church laughing and talking, rushed in for the elevation, and then left immediately again.

The reformers were opposed to the elevation, to reservation, to low mass, and to high mass without communicants. They tried to revive the primitive parish communion. Both Luther and Calvin favored the Holy Eucharist as the chief act of worship on every Lord's day. But they underestimated the immobility of the lay mind. The laity balked at weekly communion. So celebrations became less and less frequent. And while the Roman Church, influenced by Protestant teaching, decreed at the Council of Trent that the faithful should receive the Holy Communion frequently, the Protestants fell back to the medieval standard, and in Scotland many churches came to have only one communion service in a year.

The English Book of Common Prayer assumes a celebration on every Sunday and holy day. A rubric requires this of every cathedral and collegiate church. But the rubric was disregarded, and at the end of the XVII century there were only three cathedrals in England where there was even a weekly communion. The custom of a celebration every Sunday never died out completely, but in the ordinary English parish church, particularly in the XVIII century under the rule of the Whig bishops, it became general to have only a single 'sacrament Sunday' in the month. The ante-communion service, which in the pre-reformation Church was limited to week days, sufficed for the other Sundays.

We in America have inherited the XVIII century practice of late communion on the first Sunday of the month. That is probably the rule in the majority of our parishes. Shall we weep over it? By no means. It is an excellent starting point for a return to the evangelical standards of the primitive Church and for carrying through successfully what the English reformers began. Upon it we can build up the needed understanding and appreciation of the Holy Communion, and make the monthly celebration a real parochial event, a service that appeals and attracts, a parish communion in the fullest sense of the word. That is our task. Some suggestions toward its achievement will be given in the next Interleaf.

30. THE PARISH COMMUNION

THE HOLY COMMUNION is the outward and efficacious symbol of the divine unity embodied in the Church. The parish communion should gather up and sanctify every parochial activity. Its celebration should be the most interesting and significant parish event in every month. These are generalities. How work them out in detail in the average parish? How go from the ideal to the practical and develop the latent possibilities in the parish communion? A few simple suggestions follow.

The parish communion at the late hour on the first Sunday in the month may well be the occasion for important announcements and interesting parish news, including from time to time a brief report of the activities of the parochial vestry. Special prayers and thanksgivings can supplement the more formal prayers of the liturgy: 'Let us pray for the eight young people of this parish who are to graduate from high school next Wednesday; let us give thanks for the safe arrival in Alaska of Miss Blank, our Sunday school teacher, who has volunteered for mission work in that field.' Community no less than parochial interests can be remembered: 'Let us pray for the success of the new housing project that has just been favorably acted on by the city council; let us give thanks for the settlement of the strike at the Riverside Mill effected last week.' Of course such intercessions and thanksgivings do not rule out the occasional mention of individual members of the parish, both the well and the sick. There should certainly be prayers for all who have been baptized, married, or buried during the preceding month, and their names should be read. The newly-confirmed should make their first communion at this service, and it is the proper time for adult baptisms. Taking a suggestion from our Protestant brethren, we might make the parish communion a special 'dedication service,' and the first Sunday in the month a 'rally Sunday.' Communicants who are unable to be present in church every week could make a point of coming on this 'sacrament Sunday,' and to those kept away by sickness or other serious cause the sacrament could be carried from the altar. The communion alms need not be appropriated to a mysterious 'rector's discretionary fund,' but could go each month to some object of general interest.

It goes without saying that the parish communion should be in fullest measure congregational. Hymns should be carefully selected and the people gradually trained to sing their part as in the *Sursum Corda* dialogue. With competent and patient leadership (not always obtainable, alas!), any village congregation can learn a simple setting like that of Merbecke.*

On Friday or Saturday preceding the parish communion a service of preparation might be held and eucharistic instruction given. Meanwhile early celebrations every Sunday will keep alive the ideal of the Lord's service on the Lord's day. These early services will acquire new significance and drawing power as the understanding of the parish communion deepens. And the added emphasis on the corporate character of eucharistic worship will

---

* John Merbecke, a Calvinist who was also the royal organist, in 1550 published an adaptation of the traditional plainsong of the mass to the new English words of the Prayer Book of Edward VI.

make a strong appeal to many who are sick of individualistic and subjective expressions of religion.

But, it may be asked, what hinders having the parish communion every Sunday? The answer is—the General Convention. For the parish communion we need an adaptation of the Prayer Book communion service to the modern situation. If the General Convention does not sanction such adaptation it is unlikely (and undesirable) that the Holy Communion should become the chief service on every Sunday in a large number of our churches. More of this later.

31. THE HOLY EUCHARIST AND THE OLD TESTAMENT

ALL THE ARGUMENTS from tradition and reason favor the Holy Eucharist as the principal service in every church on every Lord's day. But the Prayer Book creates difficulties. Several have been mentioned. Another is that a worshipper can attend every Sunday Eucharist throughout the year and yet hear only six verses of the Old Testament read (apart from the commandments and a few offertory sentences). Must we throw over the Old Testament in this wholesale way?

Originally there was always an Old Testament lesson before the epistle and gospel. The Armenian, Jacobite, and Nestorian liturgies in the East, and the Mozarabic liturgy in the West, still preserve this primitive usage. The Roman Mass had three Sunday lessons in some localities as late as 1000 A.D., and it still has Old Testament lessons on weekdays in Lent, in the Ember seasons, and on the more ancient saints' days.

The Old Testament was the Church's first Bible. It entered into the very texture of the Church in its formative period. Without it the New Testament is unintelligible. In the *Confessions of St. Augustine* there is a striking illustration of how highly the Old Testament was regarded in the early Church. When Augustine went to Ambrose, under whose influence he had been converted, to ask for guidance, what did Ambrose recommend? The Gospels?

The Epistles of St.Paul? No, the Book of Isaiah. Certainly there is nothing more sublime in the religious literature of the world than this Old Testament book, nothing better fitted to edify a young convert. And is there anything more worthy to have a place beside the gospels in the Holy Eucharist?

But the importance of the Old Testament in the Eucharist does not rest upon mere historical precedent. The great truths embedded in its pages have perennial validity. Here are some of them: (1) The unity of God—the starting point for all Christian and Catholic theology. (2) God the Creator; the material world not a negation of the divine, but the divine handiwork; and man made in the image of God. (3) A moral God. This truth, divinely revealed to the Old Testament prophets, and preached so uncompromisingly by them, is the first postulate of Christian ethics and theology. (4) God revealed in history. This distinctive Old Testament conception led logically and actually to faith in Christ's birth, death, and resurrection, the very core of the Christian creed and worship. Because the Church believed so passionately in this historical revelation it was able to defend itself successfully against attempts made in the II century, and repeatedly since, to transmute its gospel into philosophic abstractions. (5) God works through the devout remnant; thus the new Church has the divine sanction. (6) The distinctive mark of that 'true Israel' is holiness; hence the Holy Spirit, Holy Church, Holy Baptism, Holy Communion, the Holy Bible. These are six fundamental doctrines. Any Church which neglects them is untrue to its vocation. Any Church which tried to break with them would itself be broken.

The great passages of the Old Testament belong in the eucharistic lectionary. It is most unfortunate that the Reformation deprived us of them. But we can, if we will, repair the defect. The rubric provides for Matins with an Old Testament lesson before the Eucharist; or if Matins is not said, it is a simple matter to introduce an Old Testament lesson at each Eucharist just before the epistle. It could be read from the lectern by a layman.

32. THE GOSPEL IN THE LITURGY

ON EASTER even I attended a Pontifical High Mass in a Roman Catholic cathedral. This service is of course historically interesting, for it is the ancient Easter vigil, and it preserves many primitive liturgical features. It has, e.g. no introit, or creed, or *Agnus Dei*, for it antedates the period when these were introduced into the Mass. This very antiquity gave to the service a certain measure of unreality. The twelve prophecies belong to the instruction of the catechumens, but there were no catechumens. The baptismal water was blessed, but there was no baptism. The paschal candle, originally lighting up the 'great night' in the presence of the whole Christian assembly, lost its significance when it was lighted in broad daylight before a small congregation on a Saturday morning.

From thinking of the failure of the Roman Church to cultivate a living liturgical tradition, my mind wandered off to the many ways in which that great communion is a reactionary and obscurantist influence in our modern life. I recalled its hostility to the child-labor amendment, its sinister censorship of the American press and movies, its bloody hand in Spain, its self-seeking political intrigue all over the world. And then in a more Christian mood I recalled the fact that such a repudiation of the gospel is by no means a monopoly of the Roman branch of the Church and that as a matter of fact again and again the Romans have fought for the underdog. How about our own shortcomings—our alliance with a favored social and economic class, our self-indulgent living, our cut-and-dried worship, our snobbishness, our racial intolerance, our neglect of Christian unity, our ineffective missionary effort, our bankrupt Christian education, our indifference to theological learning? Such thoughts were depressing. But suddenly the Easter Alleluia rang out—'Praise ye the Lord!' and the Tract —'The truth of the Lord remaineth forever!' Then a deacon came down from the altar, knelt before the archiepiscopal throne, and held out a book for the archbishop to kiss. It was the gospel book.

That was a reassuring ceremony. Miserable sinners are we all—but still Christians—and in some degree we do pay allegiance to the risen Lord and his gospel.

The ceremonial surrounding the liturgical gospel is one of the most ancient and precious of all liturgical traditions. The gospel lectionary was the original New Testament. In the scripture reading the gospel always came after the prophecy and the epistle, in the place of honor, having the last word, so to speak, at every Eucharist. Only the gospel book could rest upon the altar. It was placed there by the deacon after a solemn procession. He read or sang from it in a special pulpit, the ambo. Incense was burnt before it. Lighted candles were held about it—to add dignity to the recitation of the words and deeds of him who is the Light of the world. In the Middle Ages gospel books were beautifully illuminated and richly bound. They were the symbol, the efficacious symbol, of the Lord himself. And throughout the Christian centuries the honor paid to the gospel has been an ever-unifying, purifying, and quickening influence within the Church.

The reformers stupidly abolished this ancient gospel ceremonial. Today most of our churches have no ambo, no procession, no gospel book, no incense, no paschal or other gospel candle. Many of our clergy minimize the gospel by rendering it unintelligibly, and with their faces to the wall. But a rubric which we owe to Bishop Cosin's wisdom requires that all the people shall stand when the gospel is announced. That significant ceremony should help us to say with St.Augustine: 'Let us hear the gospel just as if we were listening to the Lord himself present.' It is something to honor the gospel even outwardly. All is not lost so long as archbishops continue to kiss gospel books.

33. THE NECESSITY OF THE GOSPEL

IN MATTERS of religion it is always desirable to get away from playthings like 'festivals of the precious blood' and go back to acknowledged fundamentals. If we were to do that in the realm of eucharistic worship, and ask what was the meaning, in its stark reality, of the bread and wine upon the altar, the answer might be—fellowship, sacrifice, faith, sanctification of the material world. It would not be difficult to assemble quotations from the Fathers and statements of Catholic theologians describing the Eucharist from the point of view of each of these fundamental ideas.

But what is unsatisfactory in this search for fundamentals is that when we find them they are not necessarily Christian. They underlie religion in general. And the very ideas mentioned above stand out, in fact, in that great revolution which is fundamentally religion and which is so much in all our minds today—Hitlerism. Fellowship? Yes, the fellowship of all Germans as against the world is both more evident and more effective than our Christian fellowship. Sacrifice? What sacrifices have not the German people made in the last ten years, and still are making for the sake of their Reich! Faith? Not the eucharistic faith in the risen Lord and in the power of the Holy Spirit, yet a faith that removes mountains. Sanctification of the material world? That is the meaning of 'blood and soil.' What is lacking is the Christian way of life. Hate, revenge, lying, ruthless cruelty, have taken the place of justice, truth, long-suffering, mercy, pity, peace, and love. Belief in God, but rejection of Christ. An altar, but no Christian gospel upon it.

And that reminds us of the important role which the book of the gospels played in the eucharistic worship of the early Church. It had its recognized place upon the altar. Nothing else was, in fact, permitted to stand there alongside the bread and wine. One may observe this in the IX century mosaics in St.Sophia, Constantinople, recently uncovered.* And in the earlier mosaics on the four sides of the VI century Baptistery of the Orthodox at Ravenna, to take only one other example, there are four altars, on each of which one of the four Gospels is represented.

The western medieval Church abandoned this most effective

---

* For an account of these mosaics see Thomas Whittemore, *The Mosaics of St.Sophia at Istambul*, 1933 and 1936.

symbolism. The gospels read in Latin were not understood by the people. Gradually they dropped into the background, and the gospel book upon the altar gave way to the missal. And this was more than merely a changing fashion. It meant that the gospel was ceasing to play its decisive role in the life of the Church; that the sacrifice of the Mass was taking the place of the teaching of Christ; that the papacy, that pre-Hitler dictatorship, was building its monarchy on discipline rather than on love. The Reformation was an attempt, clumsy enough, to bring the gospel back to the Church. Calvin revived the teaching of Augustine which combined *the word* and the sacraments. He thought as did Augustine there should be no Eucharist at which the word was not preached. But the reaction went too far, and among Calvin's followers Sunday preaching crowded sacramental worship out. The commandments and longer *Kyrie* are a reminder of the Puritan desire to give the Communion service an ethical turn.

Neglect of the gospel is always and everywhere a threat to the Catholic faith. It may land the Church in papalism or Hitlerism, or encourage that vague emotionalism which is the curse of so much of our modern worship and preaching. Let us lay all possible emphasis on the Holy Sacrifice. It will be a bulwark against the Hitler onslaught. But we cannot afford to expel the Holy Gospel from the Holy Sacrifice, or to dissociate worship from life.

34. THE LAST GOSPEL

PRIVATE MASSES began in the VII and VIII centuries and quickly became popular. The laity liked them because they brought good luck—flourishing cabbage beds, security against lightning, cure of epilepsy, or the release of dead relatives from the pains of purgatory. And the clergy liked them because at each mass the layman brought an offering so that an increase in masses meant an increase in income. In time, however, this traffic in masses revolted the moral sense of the Church, and, from the XI century on, canons began to be enacted limiting the number of masses any priest might say in a single day. This created new difficulties. The limitation to one or even three masses a day cut down the income of the clergy, and it failed to provide a sufficient number of masses to satisfy the lay demand. So various expedients were devised. One was to use the gospel, that holy part of the Mass, as a substitute for the Mass itself. Thus Bishop Gerald of Wales tells how (in the XII century) people had come to think that gospels were 'good physic, and drove away ghosts and phantoms, and especially powerful in this way was the beginning of John.' And he goes on to relate how a certain woman wanted a priest to say a mass for her, or at least a deacon to read a gospel over her; but in the end she had to be satisfied with a sub-deacon who read two epistles; and when he took her offering he remarked 'Two epistles are certainly equal to one gospel!' By the end of the XV century the laity had persuaded many of the clergy to read this 'powerful' first chapter of John at the end of every mass. And in 1570, the year in which he created the Roman schism in England by excommunicating Queen Elizabeth, Pope Pius V made the second gospel a part of the official Roman rite.

The Anglican reformers were, of course, familiar with the superstitions which had long clung to the first chapter of St. John. (Cf. Chaucer's Prologue, line 254.) They knew it was out of place in the Mass, and that to read it there reduced the significance of the eucharistic gospel. And they had no desire to perpetuate degenerate liturgical usages in the Book of Common Prayer. This was the mind of the great Anglican divines of the XVII century, of the Non-jurors, of Seabury, and the compilers of our own Prayer Book.

But in the XIX century some of our Counter-Reformation clergy thought it would be nice to have a 'last gospel,' and now many, both clergy and laity, have become sentimentally attached to it. Whenever I criticize it in this column I receive letters of protest. The only argument I am ever offered is—'I like it'—an argument which covered our American buildings of the Ulysses Grant period with gingerbread ornamentation and which is responsible for every vulgarity that has ever crept into the liturgy.

In our day an influential group in the Roman Church are seeking
to reinterpret their rite in the light of history. So much is their
ideal like that of our Prayer Book that they are sometimes called
Anglicans by their Roman critics. They are seriously handicapped
by membership in a totalitarian church whose decrees they cannot
question. But they are learned, devout, wise, liberal. And they are
carrying on a 'liturgical movement' which really moves. The best
of them are Benedictines, who naturally prefer the liturgical practices of the VI century, the age of Benedict, to the abuses of the
late medieval period. On the other side, in Protestantism, there is a
growing appreciation of the historic liturgy. Never has the opportunity been so great to recapture the unity of all the churches by a
return to the liturgical tradition of the first centuries. In this our
Church might take a leading, or at least an honorable, part. But we
shall 'miss the bus' if we keep our eyes fixed upon Pope Pius V and
our hearts set upon gingerbread.

35. INTERCESSION

PRAISE AND ADORATION are doubtless the highest form of prayer.
But it is not always easy for the simple Christian to reach that high
tableland of spiritual experience. Intercession, on the other hand,
is the natural and almost inevitable prayer of every believer. It has
to do with the world he knows, and with the better world he hopes
for. That is why intercessions held the important place they did in
the primitive liturgies. They were the prayer of the common people who were so numerous in the early Church. At Rome they
were called the 'Prayers of the Faithful.' The deacon announced
the subject, then the people knelt and prayed in their own words,
finally the priest summed up in a short collect; then another subject was announced. Early in the Middle Ages, however, these
prayers had become more or less formalized, and, being in Latin
and thus unintelligible to the common people, they were dropped.
The gap thus created in the Mass is still there, just after the creed,

where the priest says 'Let us pray,' and no prayer follows. (Incredible as it may seem, some of our clergy are so enamored with Roman ways that they introduce this dead formality into our Prayer Book service.)

But after a time intercessions at the Mass came back again. A custom grew up called 'bidding the bedes,' i.e. praying the prayers, intercessory prayers, or invitations to intercessory prayer. They were in the vernacular, popular, informal, and corresponding to actual needs. Two sentences from a XIV century German book will illustrate their spirit: 'Pray ye God for all true craftsmen, for all common laborers, that God provide them with such labor as that thereby soul and body be sustained. Pray ye touching every ill whereby this world is beset, that God relieve it according to his grace.'

Our 'Prayer for the Church' in spite of its name represents the ancient and medieval eucharistic intercessions. It prays for many of the same things. But it lacks their simple effectiveness. And it belongs to a bygone age. The paragraph referring to 'Christian rulers' illustrates this. The medieval prayer had been 'that the princes and potentates of the world may be subjected to the Church.' But at the Reformation the Church became more or less subject to Henry VIII, Edward VI, Elizabeth, James I, Charles I and II. 'Christian kings, princes, and governors' were put in the prayer ahead of the bishops and the people, and it was obviously very important for the Church to pray that they should use their authority for 'the maintenance of God's true religion.' When our prayer was formulated there was still some point in praying for 'Christian rulers' like George Washington and George III. But today most nations are governed either in the totalitarian way by overthrowers of the Christian religion like Hitler and Stalin, or in the democratic way by presidents, prime ministers, cabinets, governors, legislatures, courts, and the votes of the people. Only a few Christian rulers like Chiang Kai-Shek and some South American despots are left. Must we pray only for them, and not for the real rulers of America and England, France and Germany? Why must our Prayer Book perpetuate the illusion that we still live in a vanished XVI or XVIII century world?

But as a matter of fact no one fixed prayer, in whatever century composed, can satisfactorily cover the whole expanse of eucharistic intercession. Times and needs change. Unemployment, for example, is an evil that has affected us all in recent years. Why not face this reality, as did the medieval Church in the petition quoted above? And because our prayer ignores the very existence of such important things as Christian education, social justice, family life, international relations, foreign and domestic missions, are we therefore never to mention them at the altar? Then there are everpresent parish interests, for which we should want to pray—this year's confirmation class, the coming city election, etc. Shall we fear to bring our religion too near to common life? And would it shock us if our Anglican worship were made more intelligible and more acceptable to the common people?

36. WINE AND WATER

EVERY LITTLE while some very zealous churchman or churchwoman detects one of the clergy pouring water into a chalice after the consecration, writes a letter of protest about it to a Church paper, and there ensues a general outcry, exactly as if the offending priest had been prying loose one of the larger foundation stones of the Catholic faith. It is true the priest was not following the rubrical directions of the Prayer Book. But everybody breaks rubrics. And it can be argued that Bishop Cosin, who was not much of a liturgiologist, made a mistake when he inserted this particular rubric in the Prayer Book of 1662. Moreover, common sense would seem to indicate that when a priest finds there is not enough wine left in the chalice to administer to an unexpectedly large number of communicants, he should dilute the wine with water rather than inconvenience the whole congregation by going back and reading a large section of the Prayer of Consecration over again. Those who object argue that the water in some way contaminates and degrades the consecrated wine. Common sense again might say that pure water does not contaminate or degrade anything. And if a sort of struggle takes place, as they sometimes suggest, between consecrated and unconsecrated substances, why should unconsecrated water be so powerful as to overcome consecrated wine, and not vice-versa?

The offending priest has not only the argument from common sense on his side, but the authority of the whole ancient and orthodox tradition of the Church as well. In the early period the 'one bread' (of which St.Paul speaks) and the one cup, '*the* cup' which our Lord took in the night in which he was betrayed, were symbols of the unity of the Church. In ancient representations of the Holy Communion there is always only *one* cup upon the altar. But when communicants became numerous, and the wine in the one cup did not suffice, other cups containing unconsecrated wine were brought to the altar into each of which some of the consecrated wine was poured. Sometimes a fragment of consecrated bread was used to consecrate the wine. This happened on Good Friday, when, there being no celebration of the Holy Communion, a fragment of the presanctified host reserved from the previous day was dropped into the cup to consecrate the wine for the people's communion. This 'consecration by contact' was the general practice and teaching of the Church down to the XIII century. But then the scholastic theologians, with their love of words and philosophical abstractions, developed their theory of consecration by formula and claimed that it alone was orthodox. Cosin's rubric is a reflection of that scholastic theory. It became the recognized doctrine of the Roman Church. But the older teaching survived in that Church even in the Counter-Reformation period; in fact it is to be found in the XVII century in the writings of the great French preacher and theologian, Bossuet.

All this has some bearing on one of the minor ceremonies attached to the Eucharist, the ablutions. It is not uncommon for our clergy to pour wine into the chalice for a first ablution. However, if this wine becomes consecrated by contact with the consecrated wine already in the chalice it cannot serve that purpose. What can be better for ablution as a matter of fact than pure water? Here common sense would seem again to be in agreement with ancient tradition and in disagreement with the rubrics of the Roman Mass.

37. How to Celebrate the Holy Communion

The following notes are written because so many of the clergy have asked for advice on the subject.

Eucharistic ceremonial should demonstrate and clarify the great Christian ideas for which it stands—thanksgiving, fellowship, redemption, gospel, self-dedication, etc. It should be orderly but not mechanical or copyist. It should be intelligently traditional, but should not fall into the pit of pharasaic externality and thus make the word of God of none effect through human tradition.

These notes describe the service as conducted in the Berkeley Divinity School chapel. But they are fitted for any church, large or small. They assume a few people to say or sing the responses, a lay server who is not a mere boy, if possible an important member of the parish (perhaps the choir master), and a priest who sings—which need mean only that he can monotone his part. It follows the rubrics of the Prayer Book except at small points which no one need follow. It may be elaborated or simplified if this is properly done, and no attempt has been made to say just where hymns may be introduced (in the Berkeley chapel we sing only psalms as a rule). A knowledge of the usual vestments and altar linen is assumed. Learn to handle them gracefully and expeditiously. Also a knowledge of how in prayer the priest should raise his hands to his shoulders, etc. It may be added that genuflection is not mentioned, as being a quite modern Roman Catholic practice and out of place in an Anglican ceremony.

The *Missa Catechumenorum*. The server lights the two candles, epistle side first (reverse in extinguishing). If the priest brings the chalice to the altar he should hold it in his left hand, the right resting on the burse. He is led by the server in procession to the altar—the server carrying a well-bound prayer book held with two hands in front of him. Both priest and server bow toward the altar. The priest then goes to either side, preferably the gospel side, the server kneeling on the opposite side. In the procession, or after reaching the altar, a psalm—or an Old Testament lesson—can be read as an introit. The priest omits the Lord's Prayer, and turns to the right, facing the people as he reads the commandments from the middle of the altar, not turning back to the altar for the *Kyrie*. (However, as there is historical reason for regarding the two commandments as a litany, they *can* be read facing the altar.) The *Kyries* can be sung in the original Greek (as in the First Prayer Book of Edward VI). Always read the decalogue on Whitsunday and on the Eighteenth Sunday after Trinity. The server reads the epistle while the people of course sit. A hymn (representing the traditional gradual) may be introduced between epistle and gospel. When the priest announces the gospel to the people he should not turn back again toward the altar, for while the people are standing and singing to honor the gospel they should be shown the book from which the gospel is to be read. The gospel may well be sung on important days. When the gospel reading is ended the priest turns back to the altar, and he may kiss the gospel as he lays the altar book on the altar stand or cushion which he now carries to the middle of the altar.

The *Missa Fidelium*. As he reads the creed (which also may be sung on important days) he extends his hands and brings them together at the words 'I believe in one God,' while the people continue 'the Father Almighty.'

The priest then gives out notices, and if there is a sermon the server can lead him in procession to and from the pulpit. When the priest returns to the altar he reads an offertory sentence. The offering of the people is brought up by the vestry and handed to the server who brings it to the altar, to the priest's right. While this is being done it is very impressive to read or sing Psalm cxvi. 11–16 with verse 15 as an antiphon. If any sentences are used they should be carefully selected, and 'All things come of thee' should never be used. The priest then, according to the rubric, receives the money offering from the server who should bring it to him at his right-hand side. The priest slightly elevates it as he places it on the altar as an offering to God, covering it with a proper cloth. It is eminently fitting that the wardens and others who have brought up the collection should stand in a dignified way about the altar or the altar-rail while this is being done. Then from the epistle end of the altar he takes from the server the bread, which should never be in round stamped wafer form but always in one piece (the 'one loaf' of St.Paul) and which can be obtained if desired in unleavened form; then the wine which he mixes with water. The servers may here follow the ancient custom and bring the lavabo to the priest, pouring a little water over the priest's thumb and index finger which the priest dries with a purificator or towel, and may hold together till the second ablution. The priest then, at the middle of the altar, turning from left to right towards the people, mentions special objects for intercession and with arms extended asks their prayers for the Whole State, etc. The priest then turns right to the altar. During the first paragraph of the prayer he lays his hands upon the bread and wine, then upon the money offering which the server takes away at the end of the paragraph and places on the credence table. During the course of the prayer the priest may with discretion interpolate names—e.g. 'all bishops and other ministers'—'especially the Bishop of the Diocese,' or 'servants departed this life'—'especially our faithful organist recently deceased.' He should not pause between the words 'trouble, sorrow,' etc. At the confession he kneels with the people, then rising, pronounces the absolution, making the sign of the cross with right hand raised and two fingers erect. The Comfortable Words are said by the priest facing the people. After the Comfortable Words is an appropriate place for the *Agnus Dei*, especially in Lent, sung by the priest and people kneeling.

At the beginning of the central act of the service (the *Anaphora*) the priest turns to the altar, lays down the book, and uncovers the chalice and paten. Turning back to the people with hands spread, he begins the great Eucharistic Dialogue. (It is deplorable that so many seem ignorant of its meaning, and want to attach it to the Comfortable Words.) This most important part of the service should *always* be sung. The priest extends his hands at 'Lift up' and brings them together at 'Let us give thanks.' Turning to the altar he lifts his hands at 'It is very meet, right,' etc., bringing them together at the first 'Holy' of the *Sanctus*. During the dialogue the people should stand at the Easter season, and perhaps always. The thought of the dialogue is continued by the words 'All glory be to thee,' which continuity should find expression by making no pause or alteration in the tone of the voice. The hands should not be spread during this prayer. In many ancient liturgies the priest is directed to raise his eyes toward heaven at the words 'he gave thanks.' At the words 'we now offer unto thee' the paten and chalice should be lifted as an offering, and the priest should make the sign of the cross twice over the bread and wine as he says 'bless and sanctify,' as Cranmer's first Prayer Book did. At the words 'to be a reasonable, holy, and living sacrifice' he may bend over, making the sign of the cross on his breast. 'World without end' may be sung (the *ecphonesis*). The people should answer with a special sung Amen. The priest continues singing 'And now.' After the Lord's Prayer he kneels, and after a slight pause says the Prayer of Humble Access. At this point 'Blessed is he that cometh' is appropriate. The priest then receives standing. As he turns to the people holding a piece of consecrated bread with the fingers of his right hand over the paten, he may say the words of administration once for the whole congregation, or he may say them to each communicant or over two or three. He should not use the consecrated bread for making the sign of the cross. He should not use the purificator after each communicant receives. The people should come to the altar as individual members of the congregation and not in railfuls. They should not wait till the words 'take eat' or 'drink this' before receiving. The priest should hold the chalice by the bowl with both hands as he administers to each, encouraging the communicant to receive it from him. If any prefer not to receive from the common cup they should quietly return to their seats before it is offered to them. After covering the elements with the fair linen cloth and saying the prayer of thanksgiving, the priest can make the ablutions, or he can wait till the period prescribed in the rubric. He should use no wine, only water for the ablutions. At the *Gloria in Excelsis* he extends his hands as at the creed. If it is desirable to make the service short, substitute the *Gloria Patri* for the *Gloria in Excelsis*, which latter should never be used in Advent. Prayers of intercession can here be read for objects mentioned at the offertory, or short prayers of general character like 'Bless thou our coming in and our going forth,' etc. Turning to the people, the priest says the blessing, making the sign of the cross as at the absolution. He kneels for a moment. Then, preceded by a server, he returns as he came in. The people need not rise at this point, and should not be forced by the organist to rise. Organists seem to like to use their instruments to deprive people of the sense of the presence of God which often comes with the silence at the end of the service. A recessional hymn is especially undesirable.

IV. BAPTISM

38. BAPTISM

LOOKED AT from a purely architectural point of view the course of baptism during the Christian centuries has been from high to low estate, whereas the other great sacrament, the Holy Communion, has moved in the reverse direction. The first altars seem to have been simply wooden tables, brought in for the Lord's Supper, covered with a cloth by the deacon, and carried out after the service to be kept somewhere until they were needed again. But by the end of the Middle Ages the altar-reredos became a colossal over-hanging structure. Baptisteries, on the other hand, which were such an important feature in the architecture of the primitive churches, gradually ceased to be built. They were replaced by fonts which for long were considered as sacred as altars. But they grew less and less important until in post-reformation England babies were baptized at home from a punch bowl or a tea cup.

The importance which the early Church attached to baptism went back, of course, to the New Testament. There may be a question whether St.John iii. 5 and St.Matt. xxviii. 19 record our Lord's own words, but there is no question of the important place which baptism occupied in the Acts of the Apostles and the Pauline Epistles, and it is hard to believe that these documents do not reflect our Lord's own teaching. And the situation which the Church had to meet in the early centuries tended to magnify the importance of baptism. The elaborate initiations into pagan mysteries had their counterpart in the Christian disciplinary system as it is reflected in the 'Apostolic Tradition' of Hippolytus and the *Didascalia*.

The baptisteries, capacious as they were, must have often been too small to hold the crowds of well-trained catechumens who gathered in them for baptism on the great festivals. St.Chrysostom in 404, although he was then in the custody of the imperial guard, insisted on his right to go to St.Sophia on Easter eve to baptize his candidates. Three thousand were assembled, but soldiers broke up the service, and the ensuing violence actually stained the baptismal water with blood. We learn these details from St.Chrysostom's own account sent to Pope Innocent immediately after the event.

But the disciplinary system was too strict. The idea that the holiness of the Church must be kept intact and that there was no repentance for mortal sin made baptism something to be dreaded or at least to be postponed until death drew near. Country people left their children unbaptized because they could not bring them to the city baptistery. And when a bishop died, and before his successor was appointed, children had to die unbaptized. Furthermore, the number of new converts declined as the number of Christians increased, and the general baptism of infants which resulted sent the primitive disciplinary system into its decline, and the conversion of the barbarian tribes gave it its death blow. Bede tells us how the Christian missionaries made a bargain with the pagan king Peada that he could secure a Christian wife if he would be baptized and would in addition have all his people baptized. Such a proceeding must have been repeated many times. Thus baptism and baptisteries slowly lost their early significance.

There is much more to the story, and some reader may ask me to recommend a book in which the whole subject is adequately treated. My answer in advance must be this—that I know no scholarly, comprehensive, and up-to-date treatment of Christian baptism in any language. This is another proof of the low estate to which baptism has fallen in the modern Church.

39. EASTER AND BAPTISM

IN THE EARLY Church Easter was pre-eminently the festival of baptism. That was because of the belief that baptism re-enacted

Christ's resurrection in the individual believer. So St.Paul told the Roman Christians that having been united with Christ's death and resurrection in baptism they should die unto sin and walk in newness of life.

At Rome thousands were sometimes baptized at Easter. For months, perhaps for years, candidates were under instruction and on probation. In the last weeks of Lent came repeated 'scrutinies,' exorcisms, fastings, prayers, and then the Easter midnight vigil, when the catechumens presented themselves in the baptistery to receive the sacrament of 'illumination,' Old Testament prophecies of baptism (as they stand today in the Roman Mass) were read, psalms and litanies were sung, the paschal candle was lighted, baptism and confirmation were administered; and finally the bishop and deacons led the newly baptized, barefoot, carrying candles and robed in white, into the great church, there to join with the whole body of the faithful in the celebration of the Easter Eucharist. Eusebius tells us how Constantine 'caused torches and great wax candles to be lighted throughout all Rome that a brilliant splendor might mark this mystic vigil.' It was the 'mother of vigils,' as St.Augustine calls it, the 'great night,' *nox magna*, to use the words of a Roman bishop, the Christian New Year, the time when, some thought, Christ might return to earth again.

In the Middle Ages fewer adults were baptized, and baptism lost its ancient prestige. In the XVI century the reformers fought against Anabaptists, but they made no effort to revive baptism as a great congregational act. In the XIX century evangelicals engaged in a futile controversy over baptismal regeneration, and Anglo-Catholics, while proclaiming sacramental doctrine, did little or nothing to restore its proper dignity and status to this all-important sacrament.

We baptize adults in private, thus denying that baptism has any social implication, and in total disregard of our Lord's admonition about confessing him before men. We baptize infants semi-privately, and sometimes as a Sunday school feature. At Rome

Constantine's wife, Fausta, gave the Lateran palace to the Church, and in it a magnificent baptistery (recently excavated) was built. Those ancient baptisteries, of which that of St.John Lateran is the most famous, demonstrate the honor in which baptism was held by the first Christians, and the separation they believed baptism made between themselves and the pagan world. But in our churches the font is often a negligible feature. Why not, so long as baptism itself is neglected?

If we believe in the importance of the Church as a society, why not make as much as possible of the ceremony of initiation into that society? We cannot build baptisteries or revive the Easter vigil, but we might occasionally allow our congregations to witness the admission of new members to their fellowship, and we can dignify the baptismal service with the ceremonial aid of processions, lights, and music. And why should not every church burn a paschal candle during Easter-tide, that little ceremony which links us so significantly with the historic Church?

40. NEW LIGHT ON CHRISTIAN WORSHIP

THE ROMAN emperor Valerian was a cruel persecutor of Christians. Among his victims was Cyprian, Bishop of Carthage, who died by beheading on September 14, 258. Valerian was at that time carrying on a campaign against the Persians on the eastern frontier of his empire. He met with defeat, was captured, and put to death. One of the battles in that campaign raged around Dura on the Euphrates. Its inhabitants, hard pressed by the Persians, built an emergency earthwork against their city wall. But the wall gave way, and the city fell, about the time, possibly on the very day, of Cyprian's death.

After its fall Dura was destroyed, deserted, submerged by desert sand, and all memory of it perished. Then, quite by accident, on Christmas day 1921 a detachment of British soldiers camping nearby uncovered some remarkable frescoes which led to further search and to the discovery of this hidden city. In the years 1928–36 scientific excavations were carried on by Yale University with the financial backing of the Carnegie Foundation. Thus has it become possible for scholars to add a new and important chapter to the history of the ancient world. And to the history of the Christian Church—for this Yale expedition brought to light a Christian house of worship near the city wall, under the emergency earthwork.

We know from the New Testament that the early Christians often met in private houses. Note, e.g. the 'upper room' in the Gospels and Acts, and 'the church in thy house' in the Epistle to Philemon. Foundations of such houses dating from the III century have been unearthed in Rome. And scholars have surmised that the custom of using private houses for places of worship and church administration prevailed during the whole period of the persecutions until at the beginning of the IV century, after the conversion of Constantine, the resources of the state became available for such great basilicas as those then built in Jerusalem, Bethlehem, Rome, and Aquileia. But about the III century we no longer need to surmise. Here at Dura was one of these houses.

Before the Yale excavation, when Dura was but a name, nothing was of course known of the presence there of a church. It now appears that the Dura Christians were Greeks, possibly they came originally from Antioch, some time during the II century. Their meeting place was a small room—it seems to have been a converted kitchen—where they could worship secretly if persecution became too violent. As the community grew, they acquired the entire house. The bishop may have lived on the second story, another room was perhaps used for archives and for week-day instruction, a larger room was adapted to the Sunday congregation by tearing down a partition, and the little kitchen was turned into a baptistery, with a large font suitable for immersion. All this took place before 232, as we know from a dated inscription.

It will be seen that this church was quite simple, and more like a parish house than a church. The most interesting room is the baptistery. Its walls are covered with frescoes—Adam and Eve, David and Goliath, the Good Shepherd, our Lord curing the paralytic and saving Peter from the waves, the woman of Samaria, and a procession of light-bearing women which has been interpreted as the women at the Easter tomb, or a baptismal procession, or the wise and foolish virgins (appropriate to worshippers who expected a speedy end of the world). The interpretation of these frescoes divides scholars as much as does the interpretation of the catacomb frescoes. Probably all refer to baptism. The whole atmosphere of the room reflects oriental Christianity.

The Dura baptistery has been reconstructed, with the original frescoes on the walls, in the Yale Museum. Can there be any point of pilgrimage on this continent more appealing to lovers of Church history?

41. BAPTISTERIES

THE BAPTISTERY was the only room in the church house at Dura which had frescoes upon its walls. That was no accident. In the Church architecture of the early period baptisteries were always a special feature. At Emmaus, in the church recently excavated by the French Dominicans, a church almost as old as Dura (it may date from 250), there was an elaborate baptistery. When the Emperor Constantine won his victory at the Milvian bridge and issued the so-called Edict of Milan favoring the Christians, his wife Fausta presented the Lateran palace at Rome to the Roman bishop for a residence and cathedral, and the palace bath was converted into a baptistery. And when the Emperor tore down the palace and built the great St. John Lateran basilica on its site, he reconstructed the baptistery in basilican style, to become, what it still is, the most famous baptistery of the Western world. At Ravenna there are two beautiful baptisteries, one of which belonged to the Orthodox, the other to the Arians in the V century.

In various cities of Italy baptisteries continued to be built throughout the Middle Ages. Travellers will recall those at Pisa and Siena, and perhaps especially the baptistery across the way from the cathedral in Florence, with its bronze doors by Ghiberti which Michael Angelo declared were worthy to be the gates of Paradise. In France few baptisteries were built after the early period; and none survives in England, though a circular Norman building at Canterbury cathedral is called the baptistery. But in Germany there are a number of medieval baptisteries, such for example as the one adjoining the archiepiscopal cathedral at Trier, a beautiful circular Gothic building—most baptisteries were circular—which now serves as the parish Church of our Lady.

Baptisteries, whether they were rooms as at Dura, or independent structures as at Rome and Ravenna, always stood apart from the space devoted to worship. Why? To answer that question we must recall that the Graeco-Roman world into which the Church came was a world inhabited—so everybody believed—by innumerable devils. A horror of devils hung over the ancients somewhat as a horror of germs does over many moderns. Christians believed that devils were the instigators of polytheism, and that the idol-worshipping pagan was especially under their spell. If such a one were converted to the Christian faith he could not receive Holy Baptism until after a period of scrutiny, instruction, and the exorcism of devils, extending over two or even three years. During that time he might attend church but he must stand near the door along with the penitents and the epileptics (also possessed with devils) and with them must leave after the preliminary readings and prayers. Had he been admitted to the Holy Mysteries he would have contaminated the Holy Church and might have driven away the Holy Ghost. As Easter, the time of baptism, drew near, exorcisms increased. A theory gained currency in the III century that even the baptismal water needed exorcism. And various new methods of exorcism—breathing, salt, oil, spittle, blessed bread—found their way into the baptismal service. It is obvious that the baptistery, where these ceremonies were carried on and baptism itself administered, was a sort of isolation ward. That is why it was kept separate from the church, and why the place of the font in our churches is near the door.

There were, of course, other and better reasons for baptisteries, mentioned elsewhere. Meanwhile we may well ask ourselves if we are better off for having lost this primitive baptismal discipline. We may smile at exorcism and salt, but the Church of that early period did actually overcome paganism. How far are we getting with our easy-going ideas about baptism and church membership?

V. CEREMONIAL

42. IDEALS IN WORSHIP

WHAT SORT of services do we want? The following quotation from Father Hugh Benson's story 'In the Convent Chapel' may point the way to an answer.

"I once fell asleep in one of those fast trains from the north, and did not awake until we had reached the terminus. The last thing I had seen before falling asleep had been the quiet darkening woods and fields through which we were sliding, and it was a shock to awake in the bright, humming terminus and to drive through the crowded streets, under the electric glare from the lamps and windows. Now (in the chapel where a nun was kneeling before a tabernacle) I felt something of that sort. I seemed somehow to have stepped into a centre of busy, rushing life. I was aware that the atmosphere was charged with energy; great powers seemed to be astir, and I to be close to the whirling center of it all."

Such spiritual vitality must come, in the last analysis, out of humble and contrite hearts. It cannot be produced by an overpowering choir, or any kind of purchased energy. It cannot even be described. But there are certain ideals in worship toward which the devout and intelligent priest will aspire and strive.

1. Dignity. This is the mark of every approach to the divine presence. Words and movements should be deliberate, austere, graceful, reverent. Dignity can be attained without that distinctive Anglican vice, stiffness. The theatrical, the militaristic, the mechanical, the effortful, must be eschewed. Moments of silence

should intervene. Devotion craves quiet, and is stifled by the clamor which so often characterizes our services today.

2. Beauty. Worship is an art which requires the help of many other arts like architecture, music, and elocution. These arts can be cultivated even in churches with small resources. Modern Gothic buildings are of course a handicap. They and their furnishings almost always have the mark of the fortuitous and the ready-made. A revival of simple, honest church architecture would be a spiritual blessing. Good colored prints and plaster casts can be provided at little expense. Figured stuffs are quite as desirable as elaborately embroidered hangings. Copper, silver, and iron are as sacred as brass. Home-made woodcarving is often best. Music should be selected with competent advice. The priest ought to work at his reading as if he were to take a leading part on a stage. That lurking demon, sentimentality, must be exorcised. Strength no less than beauty belong in his sanctuary. (Psalm xcvi. 6.)

3. Dramatic symbolism. Beauty is essential to worship, but it must be beauty with a purpose, beauty which makes for edification and Christian living. A religious service is more than a beautiful picture; it is a symbolic drama of the divine redemption in which each worshipper has his part to play. The historical is not mere antiquarian precedent but the instrument of a living devotion. Among the natural auxiliaries of the beautiful are variety and novelty. The Christian Year is a great dramatic asset, and we should make more of it than we do.

4. Of, by, and for the people. The wretched medieval idea, sanctioned, alas, to some extent in our Prayer Book, that services are the monopoly of the priest, must be dropped. Singing should be congregational. Wardens and vestrymen should assist the priest at the altar, presenting the oblations, reading the lessons including the epistle (and administering the chalice?).

5. Finally, there is no one ideal way. Services must be adapted to the size of the church and other conditions of place, time, and circumstance.

43. EXITS AND ENTRANCES

'LET US enter his courts with praise,' said the psalmist. This is the spirit in which the old monastic services began. The reader said 'O Lord, open thou our lips'; the congregation answered 'And our mouth shall show forth thy praise.' Simple and logical. In worship as in everything else the way to begin is to begin. For six or seven centuries this opening held its ground. Then began a clamor (encouraged by the friars) for a preparation. So the Lord's Prayer was inserted before the versicles. There it stands (out of place) in the English Book of 1549 which grew out of the monastic offices, and in the American Prayer Book.

For the Puritans, however, this beginning was not austere enough. So the revision of 1552 introduced sentences, confession, and absolution. In England today the worshipper, entering church through a porch where a board marked 'Prohibited Degrees' tells him that he 'cannot marry his grandmother,' proceeds to his pew to be greeted by the parson with the assurance that 'when the wicked man turneth away from his wickedness he shall save his soul alive,' and after making a confession and receiving absolution is warned in the *Venite* that 'God sware in his wrath' that those 'who tempt him will not enter into his rest.' Thus the Puritans inflicted on the Church what is probably the worst introduction to a Christian service ever devised. It is depressing and its individualism is certainly far from the spirit of *common* prayer and praise.

Our American Church made an excellent move in 1789 when it placed 'The Lord is in his holy temple' at the head of the opening sentences; and another in 1928 when it dropped the 'save his soul alive' sentence altogether. But long before the 1928 revision the feeling which the monks had, and which most Protestant denominations have, that Christians ought to begin their worship with praise, had reasserted itself. So we got the 'pro'—another introduction. Then the 'pro' itself had to be introduced. To that end we have been visited for our sins with the intoned prayer or the intoned amen, emerging from the penetralia of the choir room, or the parish house, or the parish house entry, any place distant enough to lend enchantment and induce in the Sunday morning congregation a sentimental frame of mind. Seven introductions altogether, counting the prayer which the worshipper says silently on entering church! It is like the preacher struggling to get to the point through one opening paragraph after another, or the embarrassed lover who wants to pop the question but only stammers.

Our exits are usually simpler than our entrances, but it is always hard to stop. I was at a union Thanksgiving service last year where each minister had to have his fling, and there were six endings piled one on another. The Roman Mass has suffered in a quite similar way. What can we do about it? This question must go over to the next article.

44. MORE ABOUT EXITS AND ENTRANCES

How HARD it is to begin and to end can be seen in the structure of the Roman Mass. This service began originally quite simply with Old and New Testament lessons. It ended with the announcement by the deacon, '*Ite missa est*'—'You are dismissed.' (It was this word *missa* of course which gave the Mass its popular name.) Slowly in the course of the centuries beginnings and endings piled up. There are now about eight of the former and five of the latter, the newest being the vernacular prayers added by Leo XIII at the end. Some of these additions are a gain, like the introit. Others are simply confusing, like the confession and the *Gloria in Excelsis*, or downright objectionable, like the 'last gospel' at the end.

The trouble about having too many exits and entrances to any structure is that living room gets contracted. That is what happened to the Mass. As beginnings and endings grew, the Bible readings diminished, and the psalms were almost completely squeezed out. Something similar is happening to our services. We cultivate 'pros' and 'res,' and then shorten the psalms and drop the first lesson.

It is easier to point out defects than to prescribe remedies. But here are a few suggestions respectfully offered to clergy and choirmasters.

1. Always begin and end quietly.

2. Omit all processionals and recessionals. Or if habit, sentimentality, or (may it be whispered?) exhibitionism are too strongly entrenched, try occasional omission, as in Lent. A silent procession is dignified and impressive. Or why not let clergy and choir take their places individually as congregations do, and encourage a short period of silent meditation and prayer for all as the best preparation for corporate worship? However, if you *must* have processionals, beg the women singers not to look too smug. And is it necessary to warn against marching in step? It is, alas—unfortunately.

3. Do not use the Lord's Prayer as a preface. Traditionally and appropriately it should be a climax. Thus it belongs after the Prayer of Consecration in the Eucharist, and after the creed in Morning and Evening Prayer. Our last revision recognized this, but unfortunately it left the Lord's Prayer at the beginning of the Eucharist, and did not print it in its proper place in the offices.

4. The difficulty about the opening in Morning and Evening Prayer is that the Church, in the characteristic Anglican way, has never made up its mind whether it should be joyful or penitential. We can make it either. If penitential (as in Lent) there should, clearly, be no singing till after 'O Lord open thou our lips.' At that point an office hymn is appropriate and has the sanction of the usage of fourteen centuries. If you begin with praise omit the confession.

5. Do not copy medieval mistakes—like a 'last gospel.'

45. CEREMONIAL CURIOSITIES

WE ARE accustomed to think of the Roman Catholic Church as very rigid in doctrine and ceremonial. So it is, but only within limited areas. Outside what is fixed by authority there is a variety and free-

dom which might teach a lesson to many Anglicans and to members of other churches, and which gives to the Roman Church its
chief allure. If anyone doubts this let him read a little book recently published entitled *Ceremonial Curiosities*, observations
made by an English vicar, Father Edward Forse, F.R.G.S., who
for forty years has spent his vacations tramping on the European
continent. His facts are meticulously recorded, usually with the
exact date.

He describes strange costumes, from priests in frock coats,
bowler hats, and Wellington boots, to nuns in red habits and straw
hats, not to mention monks with moustaches and boy servers
dressed in blue sailor suits. In Spain and Italy two candles at high
mass are not uncommon. But at Cadiz there were not less than
seventy-eight, 'beside many electric bulbs that kept lighting in
progressive groups as the mass proceeded.' Continental altars are
often without tabernacles; and at Sisteron 'I found the Blessed
Sacrament reserved without a light in a vestry cupboard among
surplices and choir books.' At Zaragoza altars were in regular use
as 'glory holes.' At a church in Valladolid the font was a cheap
portable washing stand with iron legs and a plug at the bottom in
which the priest washed his hands after the baptism.

In Normandy statues of the saints frequently display a white silk
ribbon which a petitioner has tied round one finger of the saint as a
reminder. In the cathedral at Rimini the IHS is replaced everywhere by S and I intertwined, thus commemorating Sigismundo,
who built the cathedral, and his famous mistress, Isotta (whom he
ultimately married), while from end to end of the building there is
no reference to Jesus Christ. At Arcachon a placard declared that
Catholics, even if only temporarily resident, were dispensed from
all fasting throughout the year by the Archbishop of Bordeaux—
an inducement to tourists. And at Brussels a poster in the porch of
the cathedral announced a diocesan pilgrimage to view 'the white
tunic our Lady was wearing when Christ was born.' At St.Martin's Church, Segovia, is a glass case containing a full-sized brass

bedstead, in which lies a figure of the dead Christ, under a neatly tucked-in purple counterpane. And here is a suggestion for money raising—a church where statues, candlesticks, confessionals, chairs, altar, and pulpit were adorned with labels tied on with string stating how much was still owing on each article.

At Seville cathedral little boys carry lighted candles 'slantwise across their shoulders like municipal maces, making a fine trail of wax wherever they went across the sanctuary'; or again a group of boys in scarlet cassocks smoke cigarettes behind a pillar while canons stroll and chat during the service. A delightful chapter on 'Altar Servers in the Pyrenees' describes two ten-year olds, dressed in rochets half way down their bare knees, passing the alms basin with an eye on the priest so that they can simultaneously chant their Latin responses from wherever they are in the church, grinning at each other as each tries to ring the sanctuary bell loudest, always flinging all their energy into the divine praises. 'It is only the Spanish ethos that really *enjoys* religion,' says Father Forse. Finally, this little scene from the center of Christendom—'On April 11, 1910, a placid contadina sat on the lowest step of the high altar of St. Peter's at Rome, peacefully suckling her baby in the face of the congregation.'

46. PROFANITY IN CHURCH

ONE EVENING recently I received a special delivery letter asking if I would preach at a neighboring church where a window was to be dedicated in memory of the lately deceased rector. It was late in the evening after I had just been indulging in a delicious Welsh rarebit, and I felt inclined to accept, so much so that my imagination at once set to work on a sermon outline.

The service came on a Sunday afternoon. I arrived a few minutes ahead of time. The rector was rushing back and forth assigning various parts of the service to the clergy, giving belated instructions to the choirmaster, and pushing people in and out of the line of march. Talking and laughter added to the general confusion, and I felt as if a touchdown might be the next thing in order. Yet in spite of all these energetic preparations, the procession was ten minutes late in starting. We swung around the corner and up through the congregation behind an athletic looking youth dressed up in elaborate and absurd leather gauntlets, holding the cross against his nose and extending his right elbow high in the air as if to impress us with the theatrical character of his performance. The choir kept step in time with the music, and even some of the clergy did the same. The church was Victorian Gothic. It had been built at large cost, but every line and ornament shouted the gospel of the trivial, the pretentious, and the make-believe.

As we reached the chancel no one seemed to know where to go, but the rector waved us to our places, giving some of us last-minute instructions. The clergy arranged themselves in a fantastic group, some turning sideways, others to the altar, some on a lower, others on a higher step, four on one side and six on the other. Occasionally someone shuffled across the chancel to whisper a question or make a suggestion to somebody else. A visiting clergyman, on the assumption that the congregation was illiterate, announced the page on which the psalm was to be found, and then he failed himself to read the text of the psalm as it was printed. Another who read the lesson started for the lectern during the *Gloria Patri*, as if there were not a second to lose. He ruined the effect of his reading by dropping his voice at every comma, and he read indistinctly. The choir sang all the wrong music, and left a painful impression of self-satisfied but wholly misdirected energy. They did an Amen at the end of every read prayer. They shouted the hymns in an unsuccessful attempt to drown out the organ. One longed for a moment of quiet, but it never came—the organist kept the electric blower continuously buzzing.

Finally it was time for my sermon. I had been struggling not to enter into the spirit of the service, and now I suddenly felt how much I should be playing the part of a hypocrite if I stepped smiling into the pulpit, to speak as if the service in which we had been taking part had had something to do with religion, and to congratulate the parish on adding another vulgar memorial to their existing collection. 'I must speak my mind,' I shouted to myself. The proper text suddenly came to me—'They have profaned my sanctuary.' I looked for a Bible. There was none in the pulpit. This was the last straw. In despair I woke up. I was happy to find myself in the familiar surroundings of my study. I still held the invitation in my hand. But I decided I must decline. It was all too likely that the real service would be as bad as the nightmare had been.

47. 'COME IN, REST, AND PRAY'

MANY WHO have made the night trip from England to Germany by way of Belgium will remember having arrived at Cologne in the early hours of the morning, and having seen the great cathedral looming out of the dusk across the square from the railway station, and worshippers coming and going, women with their market baskets, workmen in overalls carrying their tools, old and young, all seeking the opportunity for a few minutes of prayer in God's house before beginning the work of the day. This procession of worshippers goes on all day long, and every day, now in war time without a doubt, as it has been doing for centuries. It is an impressive manifestation of religion, inspiring to witness and to participate in. It is the Roman Catholic Church at its best.

Now let us take a look at Anglicanism at its worst. Several years ago an American priest arrived in an English cathedral city, bought a supply of postcards which he addressed to his parishioners at home, and then went into the cathedral, where he knelt down, and taking the postcards from his pocket, began praying one by one for the individuals whose names he had written on the cards. Presently the verger tapped him on the shoulder—he must stop. After some explanation the verger withdrew. But in a few minutes he was back again, and this time he requested the priest to leave the cathedral. 'The people have complained,' he said. The priest then proceeded to the deanery, for he was to stay with the dean and to preach in the cathedral next day. The dean of course apologized for the verger. But the verger was only the deplorable product of a theory and tradition of respectability in worship which has for a long time been the curse of the Church of England. And we Americans are no better than the English—perhaps worse.

Why is it that our Anglican churches fall so far behind the Roman Catholics in attracting worshippers on week days? Signs outside advise 'Come in, rest, and pray.' But few have ever been known to accept this advice. Are our people too respectable? Are they lacking in devotion? Or are they only badly instructed? Is there anything we can do about it? I venture the following suggestions.

1. The clergy must themselves do what they ask others to do. It is easy to erect a sign giving good advice in gold letters, but example goes much further than precept.

2. We can make the church interior attractive, especially with candles, as Roman Catholics do. Empty churches are cold and forbidding to the wayfarer. A candle not only symbolizes the 'true light,' it creates a feeling of life and activity. What candle merchants call 'vigil lights' can be kept burning at a trifling cost—only two or three cents a day.

3. We can encourage the use of the church for activities allied to prayer, e.g. reading and study. Why not knitting also, contributing, perhaps, to 'Bundles for Britain'?

4. Above all we can introduce purpose into our invitation. 'Come in, rest, and pray' is too general as well as too individualistic. A special notice like the following would make more appeal: 'We are praying this week for our Church school which opens next Sunday. Will you join us?' Teachers in the Church school could undertake to visit the church for short periods during the week to pray for the pupils in their class. Posters hung in the church could give information about the Church school. A box

for offerings to meet the expense of religious education in the parish would not be amiss. And there might be simple intercession services each day. Another week the sign could be: 'Will you join us this week in praying for the unemployed in our parish?' or 'for the Church of England in its time of trial?' or 'for the English refugee children?'

48. Some Notes on Processions

THE PROCESSION is one of the most characteristic and significant of Christian ceremonies. To be a pilgrim is the vocation of the Christian. Like the children of Israel in their escape from Egypt, he is in flight from the bondage of sin and death. He is looking forward and going forward toward the Kingdom of God in this world and the world to come. To belong to the Church is to have joined the Christian procession.

In Christian art, procession is a dominant motive. We see this already in the rhythmic movement of the Ravenna mosaics. And in the medieval cathedral we are lifted into the realm of action and purpose, just as in the Greek and Roman temple we are given a sense of repose. Christian music, such as the great chorales, springs from the same root. And so does, in fact, the whole historic Christian civilization of Europe in contrast to the unchanging religious and social order of the non-Christian world. Mr.Middleton Murry even argues that Christianity begot the machine age. And if so, the swift-moving aeroplane would be our newest Christian symbol.

The sacraments are processional in character. They could not be otherwise, for they show forth him who came on earth to do the Father's will and passed through the grave and gate of death to resurrection and ascension. In the ceremonial of the two great sacraments, processions have, as a matter of fact, played an important part. In the early Church when the catechumens were baptized at Easter they went from font to altar in a festal procession. This year I attended an Easter vigil service in a Russian church, and at midnight the priest came out from the altar and led the choir and congregation, carrying candles, banners, crosses, and icons, three times around the outside of the church. This is an ancient ceremony. Rogationtide reminds us of the processional litanies begun in Gaul in the V century. The Palm Sunday procession was a dramatic event in the Middle Ages. The crusades were a gigantic procession. Today we have Salvation Army processions, and many others—survivals, revivals, and new creations, among the latter being our popular but usually rather meaningless processional hymn singing.

Processions and pilgrimages were overdone in the Middle Ages, and the Prayer Book almost ignores them. Cranmer probably meant that the Litany should be sung in procession as a prelude to the Sunday Eucharist, but we have allowed that good custom to lapse. And we think so little of public baptism that we neglect the glorious opportunity it affords for a procession to and from the font—one acolyte with a candle, another with a pitcher of water, another with a towel, followed by choir, sponsors (one carrying the baby), and the clergy. Some churches are reviving the offertory procession at the Eucharist, some have a procession at the gospel, and it is a seemly custom that the priest should be accompanied by an acolyte bearing a lighted candle when he administers the Holy Communion. At Morning Prayer, if a layman is to read the lesson, he might be conducted from his pew to the lectern and back again by a verger. And in that connection I should like to suggest that many of the clergy make a great mistake in starting toward the lectern before the choir has finished the preceding psalm or canticle. This is not only irreverent and gives an unpleasant impression of haste, but it eliminates what should be a dignified 'procession' to the important function he is about to perform. Finally, we might recall that one of the chief purposes of the ancient procession was to go to a certain church or place to pray. The priest, as being the leader in prayer, naturally went ahead of his flock. Our rule that the clergy should always go last is modern, and is in some ways unfortunate. The older practice is preserved in the Oxford and Cambridge colleges.

49. A WORD ABOUT CRUCIFERS

IF OUR Prayer Book services, as I have argued, have dramatic character, they should be rendered artistically. But this the clergy do not seem to realize. For example, I get many letters from different parts of the country saying how badly the clergy read, but I have never known one of the clergy themselves to admit that his reading could be improved. The same applies to the conduct of services. The clergy do not work at the art of public worship as an actor works at his art, or an architect at his.

These thoughts have come to me recently as I have been watching the antics of one of those crucifers of the familiar type who parade up the church alley with gauntleted hands, cross pressed against chin and nose, eyes peering into space, body stiffly leaping forward in a sort of goosestep at each beat of the music. I am hopeless of trying to open the eyes of the clergy to the absurdity and vulgarity of this performance, and to the discredit which it must bring on the Church in the eyes of people of good taste and reverent feeling. What can be done?

It occurs to me that, since the evil cannot be suppressed, the best plan would be to work toward making the crucifer's parade into a really artistic production, something like a sacred dance, for which there is, of course, considerable historic precedent. For example, instead of pressing the cross *against* the chin, the crucifer might be encouraged by the rector to balance it *on* the chin, varying the performance by balancing it on the *nose* on saints' days. Then, on very special Church festivals, he might be trained to twirl the cross and toss it into the air as drum-majors do with their batons. Such a ceremony would have the additional advantage of attracting young people to the church, a matter which is of special concern to the clergy in these indifferent times. Further interest might be secured by having the gauntlets colored green, violet, or red to correspond with the Church seasons. This would involve some extra expense, but the rectors of our larger congregations would be sure to know sentimental and well-to-do ladies who would be glad to pay and do their bit in this way for the Church.

It further occurs to me that it is dull for our crucifers to proceed straight ahead at a uniform pace. Between the verses of the hymn they could leap zig-zag from side to side, and for this maneuver the organist could prepare special compositions which would allow variety in movement and speed. In fact, between every two or three verses of the processional hymn it might be effective if the crucifer should not go ahead in any direction; he could pause and *whirl*, an exercise which the Moslem dervishes have found to contribute greatly to religious emotion. The difficulty of training crucifers in this novel form of movement would not be insuperable: doubtless expert oriental advisers could be secured from the W.P.A. lists of the unemployed.

Needless to say I do not pose as a specialist in the dance, least of all in the religious dance. I am only making suggestions which can be worked out by wiser minds. Some of them may seem rather extreme. But the American people like extremes. And if we went far enough in the direction I have indicated, there would doubtless be a reaction. Then we might once more have crucifers who would lead our choir processions with simplicity and dignity, and without gauntlets.

50. Concerning Funerals

'WE BROUGHT nothing into this world, and it is certain we can carry nothing out.' This obvious but significant truth would seem to indicate that Christian burials ought to be as simple as possible. Such they were, generally speaking, in the early and medieval Church. Fellow Christians bore the body of the deceased to the church, then to the grave. Candles and torches were used to add solemnity. The clergy were buried in the vestments of their office, the laity in a shroud or winding sheet, or sometimes, in the late Middle Ages, in a monk's garb. The first recorded use of the word 'coffin' in our sense was in 1525, according to the Oxford Dictionary. The Prayer Book does not use the word. The rubric says, 'The earth shall be cast upon the Body by some standing by.' Coffins were not general till the XVIII century. In old New England they were often nailed together by friendly neighbors on the night before the funeral. Children brought flowers gathered from the woods and gardens. Mourners walked in procession to the grave, the bearers carrying the coffin on their shoulders. Such simplicity seems much more Christian than the display which today so often and so largely makes our funerals an affair of undertakers and florists.

The Church can do much to give Christian funerals a more Christian character. A praiseworthy attempt is that of the New Haven Clerical Association, which has recently issued a pamphlet bearing the title which stands at the head of this column. It is meant for the laity, and gives much excellent advice from which the following sentences are extracted.

Choose your funeral director now. After a death call your minister immediately. Funerals should be held in the church, and for this there is no charge. In recent years an increasing number of people are expressing a desire to be cremated rather than buried. Our Church makes no authoritative statement on this subject. The cost is approximately the same. If one wishes to be cremated after death, in some states it is necessary to express the wish in writing, having the nearest of kin witness one's signature before a notary public. Music at a funeral is desirable and appropriate, but not necessary. Some churches limit flowers to the altar. Families may request that instead of flowers a contribution be sent to some religious or charitable institution in memory of the deceased. Such a memorial is socially useful and in many ways more appropriate than the offering of a perishable bouquet or wreath. To avoid any distinction between rich and poor, some parishes provide a pall to be draped over every casket taken into the church. The Prayer Book makes no provision for any supplementary service. The 'taps' and rifle salute of a military funeral, coming at the climax of a long emotional strain, frequently proves to be too much for the mourners and induces hysterics. Services held by fraternal orders may be on the evening before the funeral, and this is often more practical, since it does not involve loss of time from work on the part of men employed during the day. A recent survey shows that 32 per cent of funerals cost under $200, 57 per cent from $200 to $500. The type of funeral should not exceed the standard of living to which the deceased and his family have been accustomed. Before arranging for funeral expenses, bills incurred in connection with sickness should be carefully considered. For spiritual consolation the Forward Movement booklet, *For Those Who Mourn,* is recommended.

51. Some Lesser Things

IF OUR Prayer Book services are, as they certainly should be, something we offer to God, then we ought to make them as nearly perfect as possible. There should be no slipshod reading, or inferior music, or careless rendering of any sort. 'Each minute and unseen part' should be studiously wrought—'for the gods see everywhere.' The tithing of mint, anise, and cummin will not be omitted even though they are not among the greater things of the law. Some lesser things in which the clergy constantly go astray may here be mentioned.

In saying or singing the Lord's Prayer, the minister should say 'Our Father,' then the people 'who art,' etc. And in the Creed the minister should say 'I believe in God,' then the people 'the Father Almighty,' etc.

The Lord's Prayer should be said as punctuated. The voice should not be dropped at the words: done, trespasses, temptation, glory.

So with the Creed. It has twelve divisions. These should come out clearly in the reading—e.g. 'Catholic Church' should not be divided from 'Communion of Saints.' Many otherwise well-trained choirs and congregations disregard this obvious rule.

At Morning and Evening Prayer the Lord's Prayer should come after the Creed except when the Confession is said. And at the beginning of the Communion office it should always be omitted. At sung Morning or Evening Prayer common sense dictates that the singing should begin with 'Glory be to the Father'—after God has opened our lips.

Choirs should not be allowed to change the wording of the Prayer Book, as e.g. by singing 'In his hands are all the corners of the earth.'

And at Evening Prayer they should not sing, 'Take not thy Holy Spirit from us,' as if it were a conclusion—it is an introduction to the prayers.

The reader of the prayers should stand through the third collect.

At the Eucharist when the gospel is announced the choir and congregation should turn toward the gospel, not toward the east wall.

In the phrase of the Nicene Creed, 'The Lord, and Giver of Life,' the comma should not be overlooked. The phrasing of the Scottish Prayer Book brings out the real meaning—'The Lord, The Giver of life.'

Hardly any Prayer Book rubric preserves a more ancient tradition than that which requires that the alms be placed on the altar *before* the oblations of bread and wine. It is extraordinary how many of the clergy disregard this rule.

The clergy understand of course that the *Sursum Corda* is the beginning of the Canon, and thus of a new part of the service. Why then do they so often read or sing it as if it belonged to the Comfortable Words? This is almost too important a matter to be listed among 'lesser things.'

If choirs wish to sing the *Agnus Dei* and the *Benedictus qui venit*

I suggest that they sing the former after the Comfortable Words and the latter after the Prayer of Humble Access.

The laity should not hold the communion wafer in their hands until the priest says, 'Take eat,' nor the cup until he says 'Drink ye.' And it would be much better if they would return to their seats after receiving, and not come and go to the altar by railfuls.

VI. ADAPTATION

52. PRAYING TRADITIONALLY

WE LIKE old houses and old furniture, but we sometimes visit a house in which the owner has collected so many antiques, Windsor chairs, Sandwich glass, bottles, hooked rugs, old warming-pans, etc., that we have the feeling we are in a museum rather than a house to inhabit. Something similar happens to liturgical services. They inherit antique features to which people become sentimentally attached, and a change may mean simply the addition of more antique features. So services tend to get out of touch with reality.

A good illustration is the Roman Mass. It has had a continuous history from the earliest times to our own day. It is the most interesting historical document in the whole field of liturgiology. No wonder scholars love it. But if we ask, is this historic service the best medium for the worship of Almighty God?—that is another question. An English writer gives this answer: 'One wonders why the Roman Mass in its present form should be the object of an almost superstitious regard, both within the Roman Communion and amongst our Latin-minded clergy. The notes of the old classical Roman rite were reticence and austerity, those notes which Edmund Bishop described as "soberness and sense." But it is hard to realize, when one is present at a modern Roman Mass, that this is the lineal descendant of the noble rite described in the earlier *Ordines Romani*. The hectic, jerky movements of the clergy (all prescribed by authority), the concentration of interest on the less cardinal moments of the Mass, the elaboration of ceremony which has neither a practical nor a symbolical purpose, but is merely a survival marking a long departed feature—all this contrasts pitifully with the stark majesty of the ancient Stational Mass, its ceremonial so eloquent of purpose, so clear cut in outline, so restrained in expression. Indeed a choral celebration in an old-fashioned Anglican cathedral, for all its lack of scientific ordering, retains more of the ancient Roman dignity and reticence than its continental contemporaries. The ancient Roman spirit is certainly more than lurking in the pages of the Pian Missal, but the ceremonial of the Congregation of Rites, together with the devotional fashions of the day, conspire to conceal it.'

We Anglicans may well be thankful that we are free from so much accumulated tradition and from the innumerable artificial regulations with which the Congregation of Rites complicates the approach to Almighty God for our Roman brethren. But do we ourselves still pray too traditionally? Our service is one of the best of all eucharistic services. It goes back to the earliest times, retains features from each century of its long history, reflects many different theologies, and thus is very appealing to the clergy and to experts. But if we eliminated some of the family heirlooms with which it is weighted down might not our beloved service be even better than it is as a house for the common variety of Christian to live in?

The great Roman Catholic liturgical scholar quoted above as saying that the Roman Mass of the early period was characterized by 'soberness and sense' applies to it these further words—simplicity, practicality, gravity, clearness, brevity, severity, freedom from sentiment. These were the characteristic virtues of the Roman people. And are not we Americans something like the old Romans? We are practical. And, along with the rest of the modern world, we find the greatest beauty in straightforward simplicity. What a gain it would be if our Prayer Book services were simpler, briefer, more logical, and easier to be understood by the uninstructed.

53. THE BOBBIO MISSAL

MOST OF US have attics or bureau drawers in which we preserve old receipted bills and cancelled checks. But our old prayer books we throw away. That is exactly what the ancients did. Students of classical antiquity have the benefit of countless business documents brought to light by modern excavations. But liturgiologists struggle vainly to reconstruct the history of early Christian worship because so few prayer books have survived from the first centuries. Thus, although we know much about the old Latin Church of North Africa from writings like those of Tertullian and St.Augustine, we have no remains of the old African liturgy. And, in fact, we do not today possess a single manuscript of a prayer book from any part of the Western Church in the first six centuries of its existence. The 'Leonine Sacramentary,' probably only a private collection of prayers, and two bishops' manuals, the 'Gelasian' and 'Gregorian' Sacramentaries, are the oldest.

One of the most interesting of these old prayer books is the 'Bobbio Missal.' It is the oldest surviving missal, i.e. the oldest book to include not only the bishop's part like a sacramentary, but also the choir parts and the scripture passages to be read by the deacons and lectors. It derives its name from the monastery at Bobbio in northern Italy where it was found at the end of the XVII century by the great French Benedictine scholar Mabillon, who took it to Paris to his own monastery, whence it was removed at the time of the French Revolution to the Bibliothèque Nationale. Some scholars have maintained that the famous Irish missionary Columbanus first brought it to Bobbio when he founded the monastery there in the year 614.

But Professor Lowe of Oxford, a great expert in palaeography, dates it in the VIII century. This is his account of its origin: 'A little over twelve hundred years ago in an obscure village somewhere on this side of the Alps an old cleric once copied a service-book. His hand was not very steady, but he wrote with a will, and meant to do a good job. His parchment was not of the best, and his penmanship showed that he was no master of the craft. He had little time, busy priest that he was, for over-care or refinements to bestow on titles and rubrics. But he could not deny himself the

pleasure of some ornamentation, so when he could he copied a
decorative initial, with results pathetic in their crudity. The old
scribe was trying to follow his original, page for page. When he
came to passages he knew by heart, such as lessons from the gospels or prophets, he often cast a mere glance at his copy, and
trusted his memory for the rest. He was a simple, downright man
—no purist in spelling or grammar. He wrote as he spoke; and he
had small regard for case or verb endings. He could not afford
many books, so he crowded into his Missal much more than
properly belonged there. And when his parchment went back on
him, he borrowed fortuitous scraps. In the centuries that have
elapsed since the writing of the Missal, many a priceless manuscript treasure has been destroyed and lost to us forever. By some
strange freak of fate, this homely copy by an obscure, unnamed
cleric has survived to puzzle and to edify us.' *

Other related manuscripts are the 'Gothic Missal' of about the
same date, now in the Vatican library, and the 'Stowe Missal' of a
hundred years later, now in the Royal Irish Academy in Dublin.
These, also, were books used by the Irish missionaries.

54. THE PRAYER BOOK AND MISSIONS

ALL INTELLIGENT missionaries realize the importance of adapting
their services to the people they desire to convert. That is what
the Jesuits of the XVI and XVII centuries (perhaps the greatest
missionaries the Christian Church has ever produced) undertook
to do in China and India, though when they proposed to translate
the Mass into Chinese the pope stopped them. That is what St.
Patrick did in Ireland. And when St.Augustine started on the
great missionary enterprise which was to result in the conversion
of England and wrote to ask Pope Gregory whether to use the
Roman or the Gallican Mass the pope according to Bede answered:

* *The Bobbio Missal*, Notes and Studies by Dom André Wilmart, E.A.
Lowe, and H.A.Wilson. London, 1924. Pp. 105–6.

'Choose from every Church, whether Roman, Gallican, or any other, those things that are pious, religious, and right.'

The three Irish and Gallican prayer books mentioned last time were all missionary books. The old cleric who transcribed the 'Bobbio Missal' may not have known how to spell, but he (or the person—perhaps St.Columbanus—from whom he copied) had the good sense to disregard precedent and compile this first missal, suitable to carry in his hand or his pocket (the manuscript is only 3½ x 7 inches in size) and to use in his evangelistic tours as he went about from village to village. To those old Irish missionaries liturgical usage was a living tradition, and prayer book uniformity seemed less important than to win souls.

Let us look at a single example. In the 'Gothic Missal' there was an introduction to the Lord's Prayer, as in our Prayer Book, but it was not an inalterable, sacrosanct formula. On Christmas eve it ran as follows: 'Approaching thee in words which our Lord Jesus Christ commanded, we pray "Our Father." ' But on Christmas day it had changed to: 'Not presuming on our own merit but in obedience to our Lord's command, we presume to say.' The next day, St.Stephen's day, it changed again: 'We hold not back from saying, as he commanded and approves.' On January first it is: 'As the Lord himself hath taught us, we confidently pray.' And on Epiphany: 'Unworthy though we are of the name of sons, we obey the Lord's command and say.'

The words of our Prayer Book formula, 'We are bold to say,' are (tell it not in Gath!) distasteful to many of the clergy and laity. However we must use these exact words at every communion service or be considered 'disloyal.' So the General Convention, or rather the Prayer Book Commission, decided in 1927.

But we may still ask whether the idea of an inalterable communion service legally imposed, that wretched heritage from the XVI and XVII centuries of Prayer Book revision by English Privy Councils, is worth this desperate loyalty? Are we actually wiser than the great men who converted northern Europe to the

Christian faith in the years 400–800? Is our 'churchmanship' superior to that of Patrick, Columbanus, Gregory, and Boniface? Must the Church pray in correct traditional forms like 'We are bold to say' (translation of the Latin *audemus dicere*) even though they sound queer in our day? Is no place left in our totalitarian world for any liturgical freedom? Can there be no spontaneity of prayer in the greatest of all prayers, the Holy Eucharist? And finally, is it possible there might be some relationship between our liturgical rigidity and our missionary deficits? Could it be that as a Church we are more concerned to keep our beautiful Anglican traditions intact than to spread the gospel?

55. ADAPTING THE PRAYER BOOK

SOME PUT the beginning of the machine age in the XVIII century, but it goes back, rather, to the XV, when the first modern machine, and the most revolutionary of all, the printing press, was invented. This machine has helped to spread ideas, and has in many ways contributed to human freedom, but it has also imposed uniformity and standardization, as machines must always do. It has served, but it has also disserved, the Church. Calvin undertook to make Christianity a religion of the printed book. Pope Pius V abolished the liturgical variety which had persisted under the protection of the old manuscripts, and by the Missal of 1570 imposed a fixed and untouchable form of worship on the whole Roman Catholic Church. And the English Parliament had already sought to accomplish the same thing for the Church of England by its successive Prayer Books and Acts of Uniformity.

There is a law of prayer (*lex orandi*) in the Church, but this law was in earlier times a law of custom, allowing for development and growth. Of the Church of the Ante-Nicene period, the Roman Catholic scholar, Dr. Adrian Fortescue, says: 'There was no absolute uniformity in prayer and ceremonial as in our Missal. The prayers were all extempore. . . There was uniformity of type rather than of detail.' He quotes Firmilian, Bishop of Caesarea, who wrote in 256: 'Concerning many divine sacraments, there are differences, nor are all things observed at Rome as at Jerusalem. Indeed in other provinces many things vary according to the differences of men and places. Yet there is no departure, because of this, from the peace and unity of the Catholic Church.' And he might have quoted Irenaeus and Augustine: 'Disagreement [as to Easter observance] confirms our agreement in the [essentials of the] faith.' From the IV century on there was an increasing standardization, but all through the Middle Ages in the western Church there were constant changes going on both in words and ceremonial.

There is a growing feeling among the clergy that the present Eucharist, with its antiquated phraseology, its lack of straightforward simplicity, etc., is not adapted to a modern congregation, especially to certain situations. In the case of the Children's Eucharist some have tried to meet the situation by setting one of the clergy behind the children to instruct them as the service proceeds. But instruction and worship are like oil and water, they will not mix, in fact they kill each other. A service so conducted is apt to accomplish the very opposite of its purpose and turn the hearts of the children away from this divine sacrament.

We simplify the Bible, Church doctrine, Church music, and such Prayer Book services as Morning Prayer, to adapt them to the young or the uninstructed. It may well be asked whether it is not reasonable and in accordance with the real mind of the Church to make a similar simplification of the Church's chief act of worship.

Is it possible to make the present Eucharist intelligible and at the same time preserve its essentials? Undoubtedly. More of this next time.

56. A Shortened Eucharist

WHILE MANY of the clergy shrink from any unauthorized deviation from the Book of Common Prayer there are others who greatly desire a simple Eucharist for use on special occasions. They feel that the practical need is so urgent and their responsibility for winning the present generation and the people at large to the Church is so great, that they should subordinate the letter of the law to the larger spiritual good as they conceive it. In any case, the question persists: *If* one were to shorten and simplify the Eucharist, what should one eliminate?

First, the commandments and the *Kyrie*. *Kyrie eleison* was a IV century Constantinopolitan cry of greeting to the Emperor or his statue, something like *Vive le Roi!* or 'Hurrah for the President!' The Christians gave it a religious interpretation, 'Mercy, Lord'—not the Lord Emperor, but the Lord Christ. The Romans took over the phrase in its Greek form and worked it into a litany. The revisers of 1552, believing the ten commandments were written literally by the finger of God, conceived the absolutely novel idea of making them a part of the Communion Service, and tied them up to the traditional *Kyrie*, translating the latter, adding 'us,' and expanding it into our Prayer Book form.

Next, the creeds, which belong to baptism, not to the Eucharist. The Nicene Creed was introduced into the Eucharist by Monophysite heretics, according to Duchesne. This usage passed from the East to Spain and Ireland, and was imposed on the Frankish Church by Charlemagne. In the year 1014 the German emperor Henry II while on a visit to Rome suggested to the pope that the creed be introduced into the Roman Mass. The pope protested, saying they had never had any heresies at Rome. But the emperor insisted. Even today the Roman Mass has a creed on Sundays and festivals only, and that is the rule of the first Prayer Book of Edward VI.

The confession and absolution are also not to be found in the primitive Eucharist. The communicant was supposed to have made his peace with God before coming to communion. If he needed reconciliation he left before the solemn celebration began. Confession at the Eucharist first came into vogue at the end of the

Middle Ages. The Comfortable Words are a Reformation addition. In our service there is abundant acknowledgment of sins, e.g. in the Prayer of Humble Access, and the communion itself is an absolution.

The *Gloria in Excelsis* was originally a Christmas feature, and for centuries was not a part of the ordinary Mass. Whether said at the beginning, as in the Roman, or at the end, as in our Eucharist, it breaks into the logical order of the service. 'The Eucharist Simplified in accordance with Ancient Tradition' (see Appendix), eliminates all these supplementary parts, and shortens the Prayer of Consecration.

There is, properly speaking, no such thing as a 'Children's Eucharist.' But a service which concentrated on essentials would be well fitted for young and old worshippers and might help both to understand the Eucharist in its fundamental significance. Thus it might be a step toward repairing the great blunder of the Protestant reformers by giving back to the Eucharist its traditional and rightful place as the chief act of worship on the Lord's day.

57. REVISION

OUR BOOK of Common Prayer is the best in the world. For four centuries it has exercised an incalculable influence for good throughout the English-speaking world. To find fault with it is an ungracious task. Yet we must remember that its great virtue is due to the fact that originally it was an adaptation of older services to the needs of its own day. That adaptation was made 390 years ago. Since then the world has changed. Controversies that influenced the old compilers and revisers are now dead. The needs of the XX century are not those of the XVI. And liturgical science has made enormous progress, even in the last twenty-five years. The time for reconsideration seems ripe. Especially is there urgent need that the Eucharist should be made intelligible and attractive to the modern congregation. Only so can we give it the place it should have in the worship of the Church. Let us examine this matter a little more in detail.

The Holy Eucharist embodies certain definite fundamental ideas. The service ought to express these ideas clearly so that the congregation can grasp them, somewhat as a theatre audience can follow the action of a great drama. Take, for example, the offering of bread and wine. This was an outstanding feature of the old liturgies. It expressed the Christian belief that the earth is the Lord's, that we owe all to him, that we need his blessing on our material as well as our spiritual existence. Each communicant brought his offering, part of which was given to the poor brethren, as we use our communion alms. In the Eastern Church the elements were, and still are, brought to the altar in an elaborate ceremony, the 'great entrance.'

How does our Prayer Book treat the offering? In a subsidiary clause of a perfectly illogical sentence. 'Almighty God who hast taught us . . . to give thanks for all men, accept our alms and oblations.' Some of the clergy pay so little attention to this clause that they remove the alms from the altar before reading it. Some ignore it by using the sentence 'All things come of thee' for the offering. Some put the oblations on the altar while the collection is proceeding, thus robbing the offering of all dignity, as well as disregarding the rubric, which preserves the ancient order. If the clergy themselves promote such confusion, what can we expect of the laity? Obviously the offering should have an independent place, outside the great intercessory prayer. And intercession itself is a fundamental eucharistic idea. If the offering were eliminated from the Prayer for the Church, the special intercessions which the new rubric provides for would lead directly up to that prayer and give greater reality to its rather formal clauses.

Forgiveness is another fundamental which our service wraps in confusion. We are called to 'humble confession,' we pray 'forgive us all that is past,' 'the Bishop if he be present' pronounces 'pardon,' we are reassured by 'comfortable words.' But, wait, we do not get off so easily! In a few minutes we hear: 'Grant that we may obtain remission of our sins,' 'that we may worthily receive,' 'we are unworthy,' and other similar phrases. That there shall be no mistake, and as if they feared the congregation would not yet be sufficiently depressed, some of the clergy at this point add the *Agnus Dei*, with its fervid appeal for 'mercy.' And others even borrow the '*non dignus*' from the Roman Catholic Mass. We may well begin to wonder if the unpardonable sin is ours. No, we are simply the victims of the medieval and Reformation obsession with sin and salvation, and of a patchwork service construction. In fact, the confession and absolution are an intrusion. The service should pass immediately from the Prayer for the Church to the *Sursum Corda*. The only revision that would be required would be to change 'shall' to 'may' in the intervening rubrics.

58. MORE REVISION

NO MAN liveth to himself. He attains his highest development, and finds his chief joy, in living as a member of a family, a neighborhood, a nation, or a Church. Christianity is a corporate religion. How strongly the primitive Christians felt this may be illustrated by a recorded saying of Fructuosus, Bishop of Tarragona, who suffered martyrdom in 259. As he was about to die, a fellow Christian who shared the general belief of that time that a martyr's prayers had special efficacy, asked to be remembered. Fructuosus refused. 'It is necessary,' he said, 'that I think of the whole Church stretching from the Orient to the Occident.'

Corporate prayer is the highest form of prayer. Better to go into one's closet and pray in secret than to pray like the hypocrites. But, better still is it to join with others in saying 'Our Father,' or to partake along with them of the 'one bread, one body.' In the Eucharist we are united not only with those who kneel with us at the altar rail, but with the whole company of the faithful throughout the world, with the blessed dead, with apostles, saints, and

martyrs, with the 'innumerable company of angels,' as well as
with 'God the judge of all, and Jesus the mediator of the new
covenant.' The more all this becomes real to us the more will we
approach the altar with befitting humility, penitence, and self-
dedication, and the more from the altar will we carry the spirit of
this 'holy fellowship' into our individual daily lives.

Such an ideal of worship characterizes many parts of our eucharistic service, notably the dialogue beginning 'Lift up your
hearts,' which, since the earliest times, has inaugurated the solemn oblation and communion. But other parts of the service have
a definitely individualistic character. In the Middle Ages, that
'period of unexampled liturgical decay,' as Father Gregory Dix
calls it, people began to go to mass to get something out of it for
themselves, or for their relatives and friends in purgatory. Our
Prayer Book inherited this individualism. Cranmer prided himself
that with the new service it would be 'every man for himself.' The
confession is of that character; it is of individual, not corporate,
sins. And when at the climax of the service the worshipper kneels
at the altar to receive communion, he is turned back upon himself
with the words 'given for *thee*,' 'preserve *thy* soul,' 'Christ died
for *thee*.'

Today this 'save your soul' approach to religion is completely
discredited. It should be eliminated from the Eucharist. There
should be intercessions, as the rubric allows, on subjects about
which the whole congregation is, or ought to be, concerned, such
as the parish and the community, missions and social justice. And
in the political sphere we should supplement the antiquated petition that God may 'direct and dispose the hearts of all Christian
rulers'; the 'rulers' today are mostly infidels, and, even if our Christian President made himself a 'ruler' with Almighty God to direct his heart, it would not solve the greatest of our political problems. To omit the confession, as has already been suggested,
would be a gain. And if in the rubric before the words of administration 'shall' were changed to 'may,' we could forget ourselves

and receive in silence. Or the priest could say simply: 'The body of our Lord Jesus Christ.' This would tell us, as St. Augustine says, that 'we are what we receive,' and would summon us to live sacrificially, as becomes 'very members incorporate of his mystical body.'

VII. UNITY

59. CHRISTIANITY OR POLYTHEISM?

THE FIRST words of the creed adopted at the Council of Nicea—
'We believe in one God'—reflect the passion for unity which characterized the primitive Church. As against polytheism and a world
given over to 'gods many and lords many' Christians held to one
God the Father of all and one Lord Jesus Christ. This divine unity
was embodied in the one Catholic Church. 'Sanctifier and sanctified are of one,' says the Epistle to the Hebrews. And the unity of
the Church found expression in the sacrament of the Lord's
Supper where the many members were 'one body, being partakers
of the one loaf' (I Cor. x. 17).

We go wrong if we think of the first Christians as united only
in a natural fellowship bound together in natural ties of country
and of interest. Their unity was rooted in the supernatural. They
were one because God is one. The Lord's Supper was a common
meal but it was much more. The table companions were participants in their Lord's death and resurrection. And the fellowship
was not limited to the local congregation of Corinth or Ephesus or
Rome. It was the mystical fellowship of the whole Church, including the martyrs (Rev. vi. 9) and other of the faithful departed, and
innumerable hosts of angels. In the corporate worship of such a
Church the individual communicant shared, but his subjective
religious experiences did not greatly matter.

The congregation were united around the altar. Hence each
church had only one altar—which is still the rule today in the unchanging East. There was one Eucharist on the first day of the
week, one chalice, and one 'president,' the bishop, with whom the
presbyters 'concelebrated.' All the baptized and their children

were present, but if any were prevented, the deacon carried to them a portion of the food from the altar and thus included them within the fellowship. When numbers increased these simple arrangements became unpractical, but at Rome for centuries the pope kept the idea of unity alive by sending to each parish within the city a portion of his communion, the 'leaven,' so that they 'might not think themselves separated,' as Innocent I. said in 416. And for long there were community masses at Rome in the larger 'station churches'—they are still mentioned in the Roman missal.

This Christian unity laid the foundation for the civilization of medieval Europe. The Papacy was its center. But the popes in time fell into the demoralization which always accompanies the possession of great power. Excommunications, crusades, and inquisitions sapped their moral authority, and in the end broke the Church into warring fragments. Unity of worship persisted till the Reformation, but more in appearance than in reality. The introduction of low mass led to the multiplication of altars—Alcuin (800) speaks of thirty in York Minster, and of masses—a pope who was Alcuin's contemporary said nine in a single day. Masses were celebrated without communicants, were purchased, were employed to ward off thunderstorms, to kill enemies, to cure sick cows, to pay off grudges. Since the Latin of the service was unintelligible to laymen their interest came more and more to center at the end of the Middle Ages in individualistic devotions outside the Mass. Even the first English Prayer Book directs the laity to 'occupy themselves with devout prayer or godly silence and meditation' during divine service. And Cranmer boasts that now 'Godly people assembled together may receive the sacrament *every man for himself.*'

Today we are in the midst of 'gods many and lords many' again—commercialism and humanism in America, fascism, communism, nationalism, and totalitarianism in Europe. This is our new polytheism. Can we find our way back to the one God and Father of Jew and German, black and white, slum-dweller and plutocrat, and to the one Lord Jesus Christ? Can we recreate the one Catholic Church? Can we rediscover the Sacrament of Unity? These questions may well move us to serious consideration and good resolutions.

60. Unity around the Altar

CAN WE make the altar once more the center of fellowship and unity for the whole Christian world, and then go on to make it the symbol and instrument of unity for the world outside the Church? How can it be done? Shall our own Church lead? These seem to me to be the most important questions we can put to ourselves at the present moment.

Does the answer lie in interdenominational communion services? That is the step that appeals, I know, to some readers. To me it makes little appeal. I never knew a deep-seated disease to be cured by a plaster, or a great social and intellectual problem to be settled by any quick and easy method. Christians have spent twelve or fifteen centuries in destroying the sacrament of unity. I cannot imagine more than the beginning of a beginning of the necessary rebuilding in our lifetime. The more haste today the less speed tomorrow, perhaps. Quick and easy methods are particularly dangerous in all reforms that have to do with long-standing devotional habits. Reform to be effective must be led by a group of clergy who are not only devout and patient as well as courageous, but who have given serious study to the problems involved—liturgical, historical, theological. Where are they to be found? Even the future clergy, the young men in our seminaries, are not receiving any adequate training in liturgiology. And if we do not know our own mind, how shall we guide our Presbyterian, Methodist, and Roman Catholic brethren? Shall the blind lead the blind? 'Slow but sure' is a pretty good rule for those who do not see clearly.

Others find the solution in high mass every Sunday morning at eleven in every parish. The Sunday morning service is certainly at the heart of the problem, and one hesitates to criticize any parish where late mass has become customary, or to discourage any individual who finds therein the satisfaction of his or her devotional needs. But the ordinary late mass is too easy, not to say too mechanical, a method to carry us very far toward our goal. It minimizes the Bible, especially in churches where the clergy persist in reading epistles and gospels toward the wall of the sanctuary. The Church stands or falls with the Bible; it is the chief bond of Christian unity; we cannot afford to minimize or neglect it. And fasting communion, on which so many of the clergy who have late mass insist, means few communicants, which is not the result we want, or perhaps no communicants at all, something which comes dangerously near to 'overthrowing the nature of the sacrament.' Such roads lead in the wrong direction.

There is another Sunday morning plan which appeals to some, namely mass and matins on alternate Sundays, often with a latent favoritism shown to the Mass by giving it the fifth Sunday of the month when there is one. This compromise seems to me far from admirable. It is neither one thing nor the other. It tries to carry water on both shoulders and to please the mass-lovers and the matins-lovers at the same time. It seems to say—perhaps the next rector will have the courage to have late mass every Sunday, and yet he may want to return to the old way of having it only once a month; let us be prepared for both emergencies. It would make everybody unhappy were it not that most congregations are too indifferent to care one way or the other.

With these negative and depressing conclusions I have come to the end of my article. Something more constructive another time, I hope.

61. A FESTIVAL OF CHRISTIAN UNITY

SCIENTISTS have explained our solar system as the outcome of a colossal explosion millions of years ago. However that may be, it is a historical fact that the 223 Christian bodies, the sectarian

planets, asteroids, comets, and shooting stars which disgrace our
American scene came from the great XVI century explosion for
which Martin Luther set off the fuse. The tragic thing is that after
Luther the various fragments, to change the metaphor, began
fighting among themselves. New points of difference developed,
the 'dissidence of dissent' became an avowed policy, sects multiplied, theological guns thundered, and contestants resorted to
poison gas. Few victories were won. But the various groups dug
in and built impregnable Maginot lines, behind which we rest
today.

But we are not happy about it. Many attempts have been made
to restore the lost unity of the Christian Church. Some of them
have been worse than failures. The well-meant approach to the
pope made by Lord Halifax and his Anglo-Catholic friends, which
led to the papal bull of September 15, 1896 condemning Anglican
orders, gave Church unity a terrific set-back. Such attempts
always founder on the vexed question of orders. Around papacy,
episcopacy, and presbyterianism, innumerable loyalties, vested
interests, prejudices, and sentimental attachments cling like barna-
cles. To argue about them is to fight over all the battles of the last
four hundred years. Who shall control? is as difficult a question
for the Church as it is for the warring nations of Europe today.

We are forced to ask, Is there no better way? And the answer is
—Yes. Argument divides. But worship unites. Though we Christians find it difficult to think and act in union we can pray together
in a real unity of the Spirit. In fact the great churches are already
united in prayer in that they all accept the Holy Eucharist as the
form of prayer prescribed by our Lord and obligatory on them all.
Without holding interdenominational communion services (which
might be as premature as Lord Halifax's ill-starred adventure) we
can make the most of our agreement in this great sacrament. As
excommunication separates so communion unites. Such theologians as St.Augustine, St.Thomas Aquinas, and Calvin reiterate the
principle that the Eucharist is in its very nature the sacrament of

unity. Among Protestants of every name there is a growing and most impressive devotion to the Holy Communion, and this has its counterpart in the 'liturgical movement' in the Roman Catholic Church. Our Church is in a favored position. A great opportunity lies before us to help our brethren, Protestant and Roman Catholic, to a greater eucharistic unity.

The Federal Council of Churches has sent out an appeal for a communion to be held in all churches throughout the nation on the first Sunday in October. It suggests that that day should be a 'rally day,' and 'an earnest effort made to secure the presence of each member of the local church at the Lord's Table. Those unable to attend because of illness or infirmity might be visited in their homes and the communion taken to them.'

The idea of such an observance of the first Sunday in October originated three years ago with the Presbyterians. For our Church to co-operate with this movement would be consistent with our negotiations for union with the Presbyterian Church, and might contribute more to Christian unity in the long run. The first Sunday in October might grow on American soil into an ecumenical festival, a new *Corpus Christi* day, and one of far greater significance than that inaugurated in the XIII century by the medieval Church.

62. A LITURGICAL LEAGUE

A SURVEY of some of our Sunday morning congregations might lead to the pessimistic conclusion that there is little interest in religion and worship among young people today. There may be justification for such pessimism in the case of a particular parish, but it is basically wrong. A report comes from a New England college of a group of undergraduates who find the college chapel services so far below their ideal that they are meeting by themselves to worship and to study worship. Perhaps that is not typical. But it is significant. There must be many such young people. Parishes should study to attract them.

The Holy Eucharist as a form of worship adapted to the young might be made irresistible. Some of the reasons for this are: (1) The young are naturally activists. They prefer deeds to words. They would rather do than be talked to. Eucharistic worship is the response to the command,—'Do this.' (2) They like corporate activity, fellowship in doing. Such is the essential character of the Eucharist—'*We* give thanks,' '*We* here offer,' '*We* continue in that holy fellowship.' (3) They crave some activity sufficiently important to require real sacrifice. At God's altar, united with Christ crucified, we 'present ourselves, our souls and bodies, to be a reasonable, holy, and living sacrifice.' The Eucharist is *the* Holy Sacrifice. (4) And activity in a promising cause. In the Eucharist we share in the triumph of Christ's 'mighty resurrection and glorious ascension.' (5) Finally, let us not forget that the young are sensitive to beauty. Nobody knows how many are alienated from the Church because they find services so monotonous, commonplace, commercialized, vulgar, sentimental. But if we allow the beauty of the liturgy, the Church year, the Bible, and our glorious musical heritage to make their full appeal it will be irresistible.

The students of the Berkeley Divinity School have been recently working out a plan to popularize the Holy Eucharist with young people. They have held a series of young people's conferences at the School which have been largely attended. Subjects discussed have been: The Eucharist in the Bible, in the Prayer Book, in the Orthodox Eastern Church, the Eucharist and World Unity, Church Unity, Parish Unity, the Eucharist as an Act of Common Worship, and as a Dynamic for Community Betterment.

Out of these conferences has come the 'Liturgical League.' It is for young people of all denominations; actually, some of the most enthusiastic participants in the Berkeley conferences were not members of the Episcopal Church. Its purpose is 'to promote the study of the Liturgy; and while encouraging loyalty of all members to their own church allegiance, and discouraging any criticism of the dogmas, polity, or usages of any church, to pray and seek for the fulfilment in due time of our Lord's prayer for his disciples that they all may be one.' Here appears another of the resources of the Eucharist—it offers a way toward Christian understanding and possible Christian unity. That, too, appeals to the young.

The next articles present a series of three Study Outlines on the Eucharist that have been used at Young People's conferences held at the Berkeley Divinity School under the auspices of the Liturgical League.

63. THOUGHT GUIDES TO THE LITURGY

I. The Importance of the Holy Eucharist

OUTLINE: Here are five reasons why Christians must consider the Holy Eucharist important.

a. It is our Lord's service, instituted in the night in which he was betrayed. He himself said, and says: 'Do this!'
b. Throughout the world and by Christians of every name, almost without exception, it is and always has been regarded as the chief act of Christian worship.
c. It expresses and embodies the primary truths of the Christian religion—the trinity, the incarnation, man's need of redemption, etc.
d. It maps out the Christian way of life—faith, prayer, consecration, fellowship, etc.
e. So it opens to the Christian the way to God. He should endeavor to understand and appreciate it. He should study it as it is formulated in the Prayer Book service, and in its historical and practical aspects.

TO ASK AND DISCUSS:

a. How do the Holy Eucharist and Morning Prayer compare?
b. Compare the Prayer Book Eucharist with that of the Eastern Orthodox Church, with the Roman Mass, and with the Communion services of the several Protestant Churches.

c. How frequently is the Eucharist celebrated in these various churches?

d. How can and does our church architecture express the importance of the Eucharist?

e. What kind of ceremonial best expresses its importance?

f. What Christian doctrines other than those mentioned above are bound up with the right understanding of the Eucharist?

g. What Christian virtues can you connect with eucharistic doctrine?

HINTS ON READING:

There are many books on the Holy Eucharist, and it is discussed in most books on Christian doctrine, often with considerable divergence of interpretation. Reports can be made on such books as are available.

64. THOUGHT GUIDES TO THE LITURGY

II. The Lord's Family at the Lord's Table

OUTLINE: To speak of the Holy Communion as if it were a family meal seems almost irreverent. No. The Lord's table is not an ordinary dining table, it is an altar, or as we sometimes call it, a holy altar, the Holy of Holies in every church.

And the Lord's family is the One, Holy, Catholic, Apostolic Church—not only our parish, but our Church in America, and the whole Christian Church throughout the world. And not only Christians now living but the blessed dead including all the Christian saints and martyrs who have ever lived. Above all, Christ the divine brother and great high priest. Thus to regard the Holy Communion as the Christian family meal is to attribute to it the greatest possible significance.

TO ASK AND DISCUSS:

a. What differences between the Church, the Christian family, and the nation, or the family of nations?

b. Compare Christian brotherhood with national brotherhood.
c. Our failures in Christian brotherhood.
d. Does our parish have the family spirit?
e. Eating together as a symbol of equality and fellowship.
f. What do we mean by the mystical body of Christ?
g. Is there any chance of the unity of all Christians?
h. Of all Christian nations?
i. How could the Holy Communion contribute to Christian unity?
j. How could Christian unity contribute to world peace?

HINTS ON READING:

References in the Gospels to our Lord eating with his disciples and to Christian brotherhood. Prayer Book references to the unity of the Christian fellowship.

A.G.Hebert, *Liturgy and Society*, pp. 191–5.
A.G.Hebert, *Parish Communion*, p. 252.

65. THOUGHT GUIDES TO THE LITURGY

III. The Holy Eucharist in the Book of Prayer

OUTLINE: Our Prayer Book service may be better understood if we divide it into parts as follows:

I. Revelation (pp. 67–71)
  (a) Bible. (b) Creed (a symbol of God's revelation in Church history—i.e. tradition). (c) Sermon (God's word applied to the present).

II. Creation (pp. 72–4)
  (a) God's lordship in the natural world (symbolically acknowledged in our offerings of bread and wine). (b) And in mankind (alms, 'the least of these my brethren,' 'all thy people,' all in any need).

III. Redemption (pp. 76–82)

The heart of the service (from 'Lift up your hearts' through the Lord's Prayer) commemorates our Lord's death for our sins and rising again for our redemption.

IV. Sanctification (pp. 75, 76, 82–4)

In our communion we are united with Christ, receive remission of sins, and offer ourselves, our souls and bodies, to be a living sacrifice. Afterwards we pray that 'we may continue in that holy fellowship,' etc.

TO ASK AND DISCUSS:

a. What is the connection between knowledge and action, and how does Christian doctrine bear on Christian living?

b. What authority have the Bible and tradition, and which is more important?

c. Is God revealed in other religions than Christianity?

d. Can we call the State as well as the Church divine?

e. 'The cross is the heart of Christianity'—discuss this statement.

f. Is Holy Communion chiefly giving or receiving?

g. What are the fruits of the Spirit?

h. Ways in which eucharistic truth can be expressed in everyday Christian living.

HINTS ON READING

Parsons and Jones, *American Prayer Book*, relevant passages.
W.G.Peck, *The Social Teaching of the Sacraments*.

VIII. MISCELLANY

66. OLD HYMNS

WE ARE proud to belong to a historic Church, but we do not make much of the fact except now and then when we try to prove that ours is the true Church because it was planted in Britain long before the time of Gregory the Great and has always been more or less independent of the popes. Actually history never proves anything, and those who by the agency of parish magazines, Sunday school text-books, tracts, and church notice boards propagate this Baron Münchausen type of Church history are discrediting the Church in the minds of the well-informed and do not prove anything except their own ignorance, or perhaps pigheadedness. What people want is a chance to love the historic Church and its historic ways just as they love old houses and old furniture. Antiques cannot command good prices unless they are genuine, and if the parish clergy want worthwhile purchasers they must offer genuine goods, not trying to manipulate Church history to prove this, that, or the other favorite thesis, but putting it before people as something worthwhile in itself. A great deal of Church history can be built around the Prayer Book, using the familiar to teach the unfamiliar. And if congregations got more of the historic background of the hymnal it would help them to 'sing with the understanding'—historic understanding—as St.Paul recommends.

Many congregations would doubtless like to learn how much they owe to Ambrose, the great saint and Bishop of Milan, who probably contributed to the structure of our Prayer Book, and in the field of hymn writing and singing was a real pioneer. There were hymns of course before his time (end of the IV century), especially in the East, but most of them had been written by the heretics, such men as Bardaisan, the Syrian 'Gnostic,' Paul, Bishop of Antioch, an 'Adoptionist,' and the better-known presbyter of Alexandria, Arius, who fought so doggedly against the Nicene Creed. Ambrose realized that it was a mistake to let the devil have all the good hymns and good tunes. So when his people at Milan were hard pressed by Arianism and by Justina, the Arian empress, he set them singing hymns of his own composition, as we are told by St.Augustine, himself one of Ambrose's converts, in his *Confessions*.

A century later Benedict, the founder of western monasticism, introduced Ambrose's hymns into the daily monastic services. Yet century after century hymns continued to bear the taint of their heretical, or unofficial, origin. They were not taken into the Mass, except for the *Gloria in Excelsis* which gradually pushed in, and the so-called 'sequences' which hymn lovers insisted on singing between the epistle and the gospel. Cranmer suppressed the sequences, and in the English Book of Common Prayer the word 'hymn' as we use it does not once occur, so that when our American forefathers in 1789 provided for hymns in our communion service they were doing a quite revolutionary thing, and doing it consciously.

In our Hymnal there is no genuine hymn of Ambrose though three are (by the same Münchausen large claim method) assigned to him. 'Come Holy Ghost' has been sung at the monastic service of 'nones' ever since the time of Benedict, and the beautiful evening hymn 'Before the ending of the day' at compline, and 'O Trinity of Blessed Light' at the Saturday vespers, almost as long. Many others of our hymns show the touch of Ambrose's inspiration.

67. More about Hymns

Martin Luther deserves to rank with St.Ambrose in the value of his contribution to the hymnody and music of the Church. Like every great leader he was both a traditionalist and an innovator. He loved the old folk songs and music, secular and religious, which flourished in the late Middle Ages in Germany as hardly anywhere else. He re-shaped this traditional material, and tied it up to the Reformation movement. 'I want the word of God,' he said, 'to be kept alive among the people by singing.' He himself wrote nearly forty hymns, and in setting them to music he had the co-operation of a real genius, Johann Walther, the organist of his Wittenberg church. Many great men followed in Luther's steps —such as the pastor, poet, and composer Nicolai, and Gerhardt, perhaps the most popular of German hymn writers. This great movement came to its supreme expression, of course, in the Bach Cantata, that 'exposition of the foundations and principles of the Christian faith—and none more searching or inexorable, deeper or more precise has ever been' says Alfred Einstein. It is interesting to learn that today when cruel persecution is falling on the Lutheran Church a great revival of chorale singing is taking place in the 'Bekenntniss' congregations.

John Calvin had none of Luther's love of poetry and music; and as he thought it necessary to have Bible sanction for every Christian activity, including worship, he not only frowned on the organ (as in fact Luther and Thomas Aquinas and the early Fathers had done) but he went back to the old tradition expressed by the Council of Braga in 503 when it voted that 'no poetical compositions other than psalms are to be sung in the church.'

It is a sad fact that at this critical period of the 'new learning' the Church of England chose to follow Calvin rather than Luther. Neglecting not only Luther but its own poets and musicians, it set its heart on metrical psalmody. For two centuries the doggerel of Sternhold and Hopkins, Tate and Brady, held the field. In 1737 when John Wesley introduced hymn singing in his S.P.G. mission in Georgia he was summoned before the grand jury. That, however, was the beginning of the end. Stubborn tradition had to crumble before such hymns as those of the great Congregationalist

Isaac Watts and the churchman Charles Wesley. Today we are even beginning to appreciate the Lutheran chorales. But bad traditions die slowly.

These stray observations are written in the hope that some layman may be stirred to a greater appreciation of his rich heritage in the hymns and music of the Church, and may think it worth while to undertake a course of reading—which would naturally include Greek hymns, Latin monastic hymns, sequences, German chorales, metrical psalms, modern hymns of the Methodist and Catholic revivals. Rectors might be persuaded to give Lenten talks on some such plan. Or congregations might sing hymns in groups, specializing one month or one Sunday in Greek hymns, another in Latin hymns, another Wesleyan, and so on, with short explanations by the rector.

As to books—Julian's *Dictionary of Hymnology* is indispensable, and should be found in every self-respecting public library. Canon Douglas' *Church Music in History and Practice* is competent, sane, up-to-date, interesting; and it lists gramophone records which could be used to illustrate talks on hymns and the musical parts of the service. Aigrain, *Religious Music*, is a good short book. And for a general background there is nothing better than *A Short History of Music* by Alfred Einstein.

68. THE CROSS, A SYMBOL of VICTORY

THE EARLY Christians used the sign of the cross in the baptism service somewhat as we do today. St.Paul wrote to the Galatians: 'God forbid that I should glory save in the cross,' and in this he was undoubtedly expressing the mind of the first Christians. And 'in all the ordinary actions of life,' wrote Tertullian in 211, 'when we eat, sleep, bathe, etc., we sign our foreheads with the sign of the cross.'

Yet, strange to say, the cross is hardly to be found in any early Christian monument or in the early frescoes of the catacombs.

The explanation usually given is that the Christians were reluctant to make a public display of the cross and thus remind themselves and the pagans of the ignominious death by crucifixion which their Lord had suffered. It is more likely that they considered the cross an unsatisfactory symbol of their fundamental gospel which was one not of the crucifixion only but of crucifixion *and* resurrection. They were determined to associate their Christ not with death but with life.

The popularity of the cross in the IV century seems to owe much to Constantine. As a young man he had lived through the Diocletian persecution. He had observed that Diocletian and all the persecuting emperors had always had to give in sooner or later to the victorious Church. He was of a religious temperament, he was an aspirant for the imperial throne, and he decided to tie up his fortunes with the Christian Church. During his desperate march on Rome to attack his rival, Maxentius, he one day saw, as his friend the Church historian Eusebius relates in his life of Constantine, a cross in the sky, on which was written 'By this sign shalt thou conquer.' Constantine pushed forward under the sign of the cross, met Maxentius at the Milvian Bridge, won a decisive victory against overwhelming odds, and became the first Christian emperor. Whether he really had some sort of a vision or later read his ideas back into the memory of those exciting days, we cannot say; but what is certain is that from that time on the cross becomes a symbol of victory, and identified as never before with the Christian faith. Constantine did for the cross something like what Hitler has done for the swastika.

Eusebius tells us further how Constantine wrote to Macarius, Bishop of Jerusalem, and ordered the temple of Venus, which stood on the site of the crucifixion, to be destroyed. 'He judged it incumbent on him,' says Eusebius, 'to render the most blessed place of the Saviour's resurrection an object of affection and veneration to all.' He built there a church to be 'the trophy of the Saviour's victory over death.' Eusebius was himself present at the dedication of this church in the year 335. Today over the apse of the Church of Santa Pudenziana in Rome can be seen a mosaic dating from the end of the IV century. In the background are the contemporary Jerusalem buildings, Constantine's church among them, and in the center there stands a huge bejewelled cross. This is Constantine's Golgotha cross (or a later reproduction of it).

In the IV and V centuries crosses multiply. A characteristic mosaic, perhaps the most beautiful of all the ancient Christian mosaics, is to be seen in the tomb of Galla Placidia in Ravenna. In it Christ is depicted as a young man, the Good Shepherd, holding the cross in his hand. This indicates that the cross had lost its painful associations and had become the symbol of life, of victory, and of pastoral leadership.

69. Ex Occidente Lux

IN ALMOST every American town of any size there stands a large church for which 'St.Obsoletus' would be a fitting name. It was built in the prosperous years of the last century, in what was then an excellent residential section. Now the tides of population have turned elsewhere. On a Sunday morning there are few worshippers. Things are kept going by the devotion of a few of the older people, and by an endowment. The great structure is something worse than an anachronism; it is a grave problem for the parish, the rector, and the diocese.

But St.Obsoletus is not simply the by-product of economic conditions which could not have been foreseen. It was a mistake from the beginning. Psychoanalysis might have revealed the fact that some of the many thousands of dollars which went into its stone and mortar, stained-glass windows, expensive brass fixtures, and the carved reredos were given less for the glory of God and the extension of his kingdom than for parish self-glorification. And the building committee was the victim of that XIX century delusion which prevailed throughout the Anglican world that

CHURCH OF ST.MARK, ST.LOUIS, MISSOURI

churches to be truly Christian (and in accordance with the Prayer Book) had to be done after the Gothic manner.

But is not Gothic the Christian architecture *par excellence*? Certainly, as it was practised in the XIII, XIV, and XV centuries. A medieval Gothic cathedral is a great creative achievement in which we Christians may well glory as we do in a Ravenna mosaic, a Botticelli madonna, or a Bach chorale. But XIX century Gothic was something fundamentally different. It was not a creation but a copy. It did not express the soul of either the XIII century or the XIX century. It was only make-believe. In England it was almost a 'racket.' If anyone thinks this is over-severe, let him read such a book as Sir Kenneth Clark's *Gothic Revival*.

Well, the mass delusion which gave us the Gothic St.Obsoletus is understandable. But what is hard to understand, and is exceedingly tragic, is that we American Episcopalians should still want to go on spending our good money in putting up Gothic churches and cathedrals. In spite of demonstrations such as that of Sir Kenneth Clark, in spite of the fact that thousands of beautiful churches, both Roman Catholic and Protestant, are being built in the modern style on the continent of Europe and even in the Church of England, we continue happy under the rule and shadow of this dead hand.

But lo! from the west comes a ray of sunlight. People from Missouri want to be shown, so we say. Now they are showing us, to judge by the Church of St.Mark, St.Louis, of which an illustration is given here. Perhaps we are at last coming to an era of common sense in church building.

A church like St.Mark's has many advantages. (1) It is modern. It seems to say that the Church has a message for today. (2) It is simple, straightforward, honest. Those are Christian virtues; they can be expressed in stones as well as in sermons. (3) It does not waste money. Gothic is notoriously a money-absorbing style. (4) It will wear well—as practical, plain things are apt to do. Not in a long time will St.Mark's have to be renamed St.Obsoletus.

70. Prayer Book and Printing Press

WHILE THE Germans are using their infernal machines to destroy civilization, other countries are commemorating the invention of the first of the great machines, set up at Mainz in Germany about the year 1440. The printing press was a Christian product, or at any rate it fitted into the scheme of Christian culture. Its first book was the Bible, and much of the work of the early printers was done for the Church. The first missal appeared in 1474, and by the time of the Reformation there were over two hundred printed diocesan missals. Among the earliest books to come from Caxton's press at Westminster was the *Directorium* or *Pie*, a sort of perpetual church almanac, of which the preface to the first Prayer Book said, 'To turn the book only was so hard and intricate a matter that many times there was more business to find out what should be read than to read it when it was found out.' Its tables and rules were, in fact, so confusing that the word 'pie' came in printing offices to be synonymous with confusion.

Machines serve man, but they also control him to a greater or less degree. The printing press traffics in words, which are inseparable from thoughts; hence its profound influence on our intellectual and spiritual progress. Luther's 'open Bible' was nothing but a translation printed in cheap form for general circulation. Similarly the printing press popularized the Prayer Book and standardized it. 'The people,' says the preface to the Book of 1549, 'shall not be at so great charge for books as in times past they have been.' Whereas 'there has been great diversity in saying and singing in churches, henceforth all the whole realm shall have but one use.' Twenty-one years later Pope Pius V issued the standard Roman Catholic missal, and thereafter any adaptation or improvement was ruled out because of the enormous expense involved. It is said that a revision of our Prayer Book would cost several million dollars. In England Prayer Books are changed to correspond with changes in the prayers for the royal family, but the new pages are inserted in books already printed. One such book had a life of only ten hours.

Printing always interprets. The capitalization of '*Hoc est corpus meum*' in the Roman Mass reflects the revolution in the theology of the Mass which occurred in the XIII century. In the XVIII century some of our Prayer Books had the Holy Communion printed in small type, thus stigmatizing it as an 'occasional' office. Psalm cv. 25 can have two different meanings, depending on whether a comma comes before or after the word 'so.' The Cambridge Press prints it before, the Oxford Press after. Printers are said to be responsible for placing the name 'Protestant Episcopal' upon the title page of our first Prayer Book, that of 1785. If so our Church would seem to be the only one in Christendom with a machine-made name.

And our American printers have imposed an important interpretation upon our Communion service by means of a capital letter. The consecratory prayer or Canon begins, of course, with the preface (which means proclamation). In all the new Anglican liturgies (see the Alcuin Club's recently published collection) this is made clear by the word 'Consecration' or '*Anaphora*' printed above the *Sursum Corda* and preface. The mistaken medieval idea was that the Canon began with the *Te igitur*, and scribes often distinguished this initial T by turning it into a crucifix or otherwise elaborately decorating it. But the first English Prayer Books did not recognize an independent 'Prayer of Consecration.' This name first appeared in Laud's book of 1637, whence it worked into the English revision of 1662, and into our own book. The large A printed in our present altar books at the beginning of this prayer sanctions the medieval mistake. 'Lift up your hearts' printed with a large L probably is quite unauthorized but it would have restrained the clergy in their bad habit of saying this phrase as if it were one of the Comfortable Words.

71. Educating the Clergy

ONE OF THE features of the *Manchester Guardian Weekly* is a religious column written by 'Artifex.' Recently it discussed the 'parson's reading,' giving much excellent advice on this exceedingly important subject. But at the end came this recommendation—study dogmatics first, Church history next, then ethics, psychology, ecclesiology, comparative religion. The omission of the Bible was surprising. But it was less surprising that Artifex should omit the Prayer Book, for few churchmen either in England or America seem to think liturgiology a subject of any urgent importance. (Perhaps he meant it to be included under 'ecclesiology.')

What the parson should read raises the whole question of the education of the clergy. One would suppose it was obvious that all education had the good life as its end and aim. But the college professors have, as usual, confused our thinking, and have in fact buried the fundamental issue out of sight. They exalt theoretical knowledge, loading their teaching with formulas, arguments, facts, and graphs. But about the good life they have little or nothing to say. To mention it in the classroom would be unscientific, almost unethical. And many of our clergy and laity, having become pessimistic about the Church, seem to think that everything would improve if these professional principles could be applied to theological education. The idea seems to be that when a young man has acquired the requisite number of college credits so that he can annex the mystic letters B.A. (not to his sweater but to his name), and then by means of other credits, acquired in a theological seminary, can put B.D. after B.A., he has become equipped to assume the cure of immortal souls in the Church of God. The only question is about the right curriculum, which in accordance with the spirit of the age must be replete with practical courses. Thus spake the commission of eminent bishops, presbyters, and laymen in their report on theological seminaries to our last General Convention, which report, so far as I can recall, hardly mentioned Christian living or the way by which the candidate for the ministry was to attain it.

Of course so long as we think of preparation for Holy Orders in terms of curricula and degrees the good life does get crowded out. For it cannot be engendered by any juggling of curricula or marks or diplomas. It has to be won if at all by rigid self-discipline in a community which is permeated with the spirit of the Christian religion. The good life for the theological student involves an adequate training in Bible, dogmatics, and the rest of Artifex's list. But such studies if they are to be good must be approached from the vantage ground of a living faith. St. Thomas Aquinas on his knees found out the truth about God, and it is still the best way. Theological learning must begin, so to speak, at the altar. Personal devotion, which Artifex urges, is all-important, but it is not to be transmitted by classroom processes. What can be taught is the history and contents of the Prayer Book, reverent reading and singing, the art of corporate worship, liturgical instinct.

In short, liturgiology, far from being a sort of extra or specialty, is at the very heart of the theological curriculum, and is an essential subject of study for parsons as for seminarians. And it is largely because this fact has been ignored that our Anglican standards of worship remain so low, and that in both America and England the well-informed layman as well as the man in the street so often observes Sunday in some other way than by going to church.

72. SOME STRAY THOUGHTS

IT IS always profitable to see ourselves as others see us, and to listen to intelligent criticism. Professor James Bissett Pratt of Williams College is well known to the American public for his many books on religious psychology and philosophy. He is not an Episcopalian, but he has been for many years an attendant at our services. In answer to an inquirer he recently sent the following 'stray thoughts,' as he calls them, which he has given permission to publish in this column:

While performing the ritual properly, the priest should certainly be as inconspicuous as he can. His bodily presence is needed, but his own particular personality should not intrude. In reading the Scripture, the prayers, etc., while he should not use an expressionless voice, he should beware of too great inflections and too much stress, and should strive to let the texts speak for themselves.

As you know my book, and its chapters on worship, you know in a general way my views of the mechanics of the service. The Episcopal Church comes nearer the golden mean, in my opinion, than either the Roman or the ultra-Protestant. The weakest spot in the service in your Church is usually the sermon: both because it is so often neglected and because in so many cases the rather superficial remarks of the priest are delivered in a pompous and tremendous tone, as if he thought he were saying something of profound importance and great originality.

There is one small change which I should like to see tried (though I doubt if I shall ever see it), and that is that the congregation remain seated whenever the choir sings something in which the congregation is not expected to join—e.g. the anthem, or the *Te Deum*. I say this because it is the worshipful, the contemplative, attitude of mind which is, at the time, desired; and standing is the least contemplative of bodily attitudes. For successful contemplation, the merging of the individual with the Divine, one needs relaxed muscles, but the erect posture predisposes one to the strenuous, the active attitude of mind, and produces sensations which force themselves upon one's notice. I always find my own worship in your Church noticeably interfered with by the standing attitude. There are parts of the service where the strenuous mood is proper, e.g. in the creed and the hymns, and here the congregation should stand. But not all the Church service should be strenuous, self-conscious, and militant.

I might add that personally I have never found anything valuable in responsive readings. It is not a worshipful performance, it is neither contemplative, nor morally strenuous—a kind of reading lesson—and in your Church too often a kind of race. I also wish we might have more *silence*.

There may be a question about some of these points, but there can be no doubt that many of our clergy need elocution lessons; and if their sermons are so poor it must be because they have nothing of vital importance to say. So the hungry sheep look up and are not fed. Perhaps one thing that keeps the clergy back is having too many unintelligent admirers, and too few intelligent critics.

73. FRAGMENTS

APPEAL TO CHRISTIAN BRETHREN. Unity is in the air in the Church and is the great need in the world outside. I am proposing here that the Christian Church should take the present opportunity to return to unity through worship; that all Christians should make the Holy Communion the center of the Lord's day, as it was in the first Christian centuries. In those days the Lord's Supper was 'a sacrament of unity, the Christian family meal, the chief community service on each Lord's day.' This custom continued—the most ancient tradition of the Church—until the Reformation. Luther himself indeed believed this strongly. (His idea was to accept everything from the medieval Church that the Bible did not forbid. Therefore the Lutheran Church has hymns, candles, crucifix—with an emphasis on art and beauty.) Calvin was more concerned for the word, for preaching, but he also thought the Holy Communion should be the central act of devotion every Sunday. Unfortunately the next generation of Protestants preferred to adopt the ideas of Zwingli, who was more radical and who had a barren and sentimental attitude toward religion; and therefore the ancient tradition of the Church was rejected, the weekly celebration of the Holy Communion was given up, and with it the belief that it was the most important corporate act of the Christian community. The causes for this were of course many and various. Some have been outlined in the Interleaf 'Luther and the Mass.' Moreover, superstitions had gathered around the Holy Communion, such as the elevation of the host; it had become Christocentric; futile controversies had developed over the real meaning of the presence. But today liturgical reformers in all churches find a certain fundamental similarity in their ideas. This is an age of sacramentalism (e.g. Communism and Nazism with their use of symbols); and we have before us a great opportunity to return to the Holy Eucharist. Professor Tillich, one of the greatest of Protestant scholars, says 'Protestantism as a church for the masses can continue to exist only if it is able to undergo a fundamental change. In order to do this it must obtain a new understanding of symbols and of sacraments.' All Christians can agree in regarding the Holy Communion as the central act of their religion and the symbol of their brotherhood, and thus achieve a practical expression of unity which is better than the controversial appeal to orders.*

WHY THE LAITY PREFER MORNING AND EVENING PRAYER TO THE EUCHARIST. One answer might be that they do not. But the history of the last four hundred years makes the fact undeniable. Since Cranmer's time a considerable majority of our churches have Morning Prayer for their chief service on Sunday morning, and consequently the laity have attended Morning Prayer to the neglect of the Holy Communion as the chief act of Sunday worship. (The early Wesleyans, whose sacramental sense was strong, formed a noteworthy exception.) In spite of the great efforts made in the last seventy-five years to replace matins by the 'mass,' church statistics show that the same state of affairs exists today. There is a certain justification for it in that the choir offices (i.e.

* The Liturgical League, q.v., is an organization formed to practise the ideas outlined above.

Morning and Evening Prayer) are laymen's services, arranged by St.Benedict, a layman, for the use of laymen. But there are many other reasons for the layman's neglect of the Holy Eucharist, and most of them are due not to qualities inherent in the liturgy, but to unfortunate accretions of ceremonial and misinterpretations which are now under fire from liturgical experts in all the churches.

The Holy Eucharist is regarded, for instance, as too complicated and theological for the layman to understand. Throughout the service he is given far too little to do; in fact he is sometimes discouraged from even knowing what is going on at the altar. There is too little variety; too much kneeling, for example, especially for women or the aged, who find it physically very trying.

Nowadays, moreover, many lay people think the Holy Communion is gloomy (in strange contrast to its early meaning of Eucharist, i.e. Thanksgiving). Or they find it too awe-inspiring and mysterious; and they fear that if it were too frequently celebrated it might be cheapened. Along with this goes the idea that there is need of long preparation for communion.

As a matter of fact, much that belongs properly to the Eucharist has been incorporated in the choir offices—the sermon, offering, penitential introduction, and intercessions. Also, the offices give an important place to the Old Testament, of which there is entirely too little in our present eucharistic lectionary.

With the increased understanding of the liturgy and the trend toward corporate rather than individualistic devotions, these faults can be set right, so that there ought no longer to be any reason why the modern Church should not follow the ancient tradition of the Church and celebrate the Lord's Supper as the chief service of the Lord's day.

OLD AND NEW PRAYERS IN THE PRAYER BOOK. A modern and scholarly book on the source and atmosphere of the Prayer Book prayers would make a fascinating study. Cranmer, that great liturgiologist, and his helpers translated many of the prayers from the Latin and others they composed afresh. Many of these can be identified. It was a great literary age, and much of the beauty of the Prayer Book prayers is due to these men and to their followers in the XVII century—e.g. Jeremy Taylor's magnificent prayer for the visitation of the sick (p. 314).

In the XIX and XX centuries we have undertaken to enrich the Prayer Book. The *Times Literary Supplement* lately commended as one of the best modern prayers 'Remember O Lord what Thou hast wrought in us.' But it is not modern: it is a translation by Bishop Paget of the *Domine quod es operatus* from the Leonine Sacramentary. However, such deft hands as those of Bishop Paget, Dean Church, or Cardinal Newman (it will be recalled that he was almost officially called on to translate some of the Roman service books) have given us great prayers equal to some of the old. But it was a romantic period, and romantics always write much tosh. Keble and his group produced mostly bric-à-brac. Today, we have outgrown romanticism. Today we demand reality, objectivity, simplicity, and straightforwardness, expressed in exact language.* Winston Churchill's speeches are a model of this kind of writing. It is the way to speak and, one may add, to preach and pray, to reach the man in the street. Let us look at one or two of our modern prayers in the light of this standard.

The section entitled Family Prayer in the Prayer Book gives some glaring examples of what prayers should not be; but perhaps the oft-used General Intercession on page 592 is the worst. In content it is insincere; in expression pretentious and artificial. Archaisms and circumlocutions combine to give it an air of falsity. It is evidently the product of an uneasy feeling that the Church should be concerned for social justice, but not of an ardent conviction that churchmen should themselves do anything about it. We piously hope that by miraculous intervention God will prevent the withholding of wages, but we do not care enough about it to feel under obligation to help pass laws to that effect. Instead of working for prison reform we salve our consciences by describ-

* See T.E. Hulme, *Speculations*, for the development of this idea.

ing the lot of prisoners in a phrase that, though it has dignity in its original place in the Psalms, sounds weak and sentimental here. As for the last sentence, what does it mean? Are we not all appointed to die?

These remarks may seem hypercritical, but it is well that we should realize it is a serious offense to admit to our Prayer Book anything that is not of the highest quality from the literary as well as the religious point of view.

DRAMA. Every great movement gains popular adherence by dramatization. So it is in modern Communism and in the Nazi Reich. Through drama they appeal to popular imagination. This is as true of religion as of politics. The theatre in ancient Athens was as closely linked to religion as the medieval stage. . .

The Hebrews dramatized their history in the seasonal festivals. The Passover ritual, for example, recalled the time when the Hebrews went forth out of Egypt across the Red Sea under Moses. This was a drama of humanity going forth from the bondage of sin to the land of promise. Christianity took over and greatly expanded such dramatization—from the fall of the angels before history to the final consummation of history. It had no other way to explain sin and redemption. We cannot understand history, we cannot understand nature in any other way, than as drama. We are not interested in history as mere facts.

The central act of the Christian drama, of course, was the death and resurrection of Jesus Christ. This the Eucharist expressed. It is right then to speak of the Holy Eucharist as drama.

OBLIGATION. Discipline is needed in order to accomplish anything. The Reformation reacted against the excessive discipline and rule and law of the medieval Church, substituting preaching, confidence in the *word*. It believed in a discipline of life, but not of prayer, i.e. the obligation to perform religious duties. These ideas however do not work. Look at the world today. The great new religions of Antichrist (Nazism and Communism) owe their enormous influence to the discipline not only of life but of thought that they impose. That the young people of today welcome such discipline is shown by the fact that these movements are largely supported by the young.

The Roman Church sets us the same example. No one but is impressed with the church-going Roman Catholic population and with the loyalty of their young people. They are under obligation. Contrast our Church. We lose the young. We demand nothing from them. We need to instil in them the idea of obligation. This, rather than the provision of recreation, is the function of Young People's Fellowships.

MATERIAL AND SPIRITUAL. In the beginning God created heaven and earth. The Old Testament never forgot that. The *earth* is the Lord's—not simply heaven. So there was a place for the beauty of the world in its worship. In the early Christian era the tendency of Greek religious thinkers was in contrast to this. They endeavored to escape from the body and create a spiritual religion detached from the material world and things of sense.

But the Christian Church inherited the Jewish point of view, and its great contest with the heresy of Gnosticism—called by Harnack 'the acute Hellenization' of Christianity—concerned the faith in God as creator and the Word made flesh. Thus the Church expressed in its worship, the Holy Eucharist, its belief that in the bread of the fields and the wine of the vineyards the body and soul are fed. Irenaeus, the great II century Father, and opponent of the Gnostics, said, 'We offer to him his own, announcing consistently the fellowship and union of the flesh and Spirit.'

Today he who truly enters into eucharistic worship cannot be indifferent to hunger, bad housing, and other material and social evils. . . See *The Social Teaching of the Sacraments*, by W.G.Peck.

THE ANGLICAN COUNTER-REFORMATION. Now that a hundred years have passed since the beginning of the Oxford Movement, it is possible to evaluate some of its effects. In spite of its pro-Romanism and its many converts to Rome it has done nothing to close the breach. The breach is wider perhaps. Its scorn of low churchmen has bitterly alienated not only churchmen but also the nonconformists. It has on the whole failed to reach the middle class and slum dwellers. It has produced a strange combination of individualistic piety and submission of the individual, but no vital social gospel; in the liturgy, concern with presence rather than with offering; attempts to conform to the Roman Mass and Roman ceremonial with no good results; rigid standardization of worship; no parish communion; eucharistic adoration. . .

Christian socialists among present-day Anglo-Catholics are aware of many of these errors and are seeking valiantly to overcome them. See, for example, Father A.G.Hebert's recent books *Liturgy and Society* and *The Parish Communion.*

THE CHURCH has made gigantic mistakes and cherished others, has been often on the side of wrong. The strange thing is that this surprises, upsets some people and alienates them from the Church. But where do they look for the ark of salvation? In politics, press, or education? The defense of the Church is that it has an ideal—perfection. And by its very nature it claims the right to demand perfection of its adherents and to preach it to the world.

IX. QUESTION BOX

When these Interleaves first appeared questions were invited and many were received. Some of the most interesting are here reprinted.

Q. SHOULD the priest stand at the suffrages and collects in Morning and Evening Prayer? A. The statement reiterated so often in our ill-informed books of devotion that we should always kneel for prayer and stand for praise is quite mistaken. The early way was to stand for prayer. 'When ye *stand* praying,' said our Lord (St.Mark xi. 25). In the early Church the people always stood praying on Sundays, and during the period from Easter to Pentecost on weekdays as well. The catacombs have many representations of figures standing and praying—the *orantes*. To stand in prayer is the generally accepted custom in the Eastern Orthodox Church. In our Church this custom survives in the Eucharist, where the priest stands except for the confession. Both before and after the Reformation in England the minister stood during the suffrages and collects. But by the time of the 1662 revision of the Prayer Book congregations had grown slack, owing to Puritan influence, and remained sitting during the prayers. Accordingly a rubric was inserted just before the collects in Morning Prayer which said 'all kneeling,' i.e. all the people kneeling. In America this rubric was wrongly understood as including the minister. The revised rubric in our present Prayer Book seems to indicate clearly that while the people kneel the minister should remain standing after the creed through the suffrages and collects. Perhaps he should follow the English custom and kneel during the Lord's Prayer when it is said at this place.

Q. The *Gloria in Excelsis* lengthens the post-communion so much that some of my people leave church before the end of the service. Might it not better come after the *Kyrie,* as in the Roman Mass? A. The *Kyries* at the beginning of the communion service are the remnant of a litany which included all sorts of intercessions similar to those in our Prayer for the Church. The collect followed these intercessions, and thus 'collected' the intercessions of the congregation in a single prayer. Our commandments, coming between the *Kyries* and the collect, are obviously out of place. So is the *Gloria in Excelsis* in the Roman Mass. 'Its insertion here is to be regretted,' says the great Roman Catholic liturgist, Dom Cabrol. One might add a regret that some of our clergy seem to think it nice to copy this Roman blunder. If a shorter postcommunion is desired, a good way is to sing the *Gloria Patri* to some familiar melody in place of the *Gloria in Excelsis.*

Q. Our parish desires to make a new surplice for the rector, but finds the price of linen at the present time prohibitive. Would it be allowable to make a surplice of some other material? A. There is nothing sacred about linen. Its ecclesiastical use came from the fact that it was the most available material, and cotton was rare in the northern churches. The Eastern Church has long used silk to cover the altar vessels and for clergy vestments. The war interferes with the export of Russian flax, so the price of linen is likely to remain high for some time to come. There is no reason why we should not experiment with rayon, celanese, and other materials. Home-made things are best, and it would be a great gain if all our churches could refrain in these difficult days from lavish and unnecessary expenditure on the material side of worship. Some of the clergy are training their people to make beautiful colored vestments and altar hangings out of all sorts of inexpensive materials.

Q. Why do you object to using the sentence 'All things come of thee' at the Eucharist? A. Because the Prayer for the Church provides for offering the alms. To say this sentence beforehand is to deprive the prescribed offering of all significance and make it one of those 'vain repetitions' which our Lord condemned.

Q. Referring to your comment on Whitsunday, is it not true that the *Epiclesis* (invocation) theory is rapidly going out of fashion? A. There are many *Epiclesis* theories. I was not concerned with theory but with fact. The fact is that the primitive Eucharist not only recognized God the creator and Christ the redeemer but gave the fullest recognition to the life-giving Spirit who makes the divine creation and redemption a reality to the worshipper. The medieval Church lost this idea, hence the absence of the Holy Spirit from the Roman Mass and the English Communion service. We are fortunate in having not only the Sarum prayer 'Cleanse the thoughts of our hearts by the inspiration of thy Holy Spirit,' but the invocation of the Holy Spirit in our Prayer of Consecration.

Q. Funerals frequently bring out the worst traits in human nature. Will you not say something in your column about keeping the casket open during the service? A. In answer I cannot do better than to quote some further sentences from the letter of this correspondent. 'Ten years ago most undertakers wanted the casket kept open because it advertized the rapidly developing science of embalming. But now embalming is so universal that the difference between one undertaker's ability to embalm and another's is usually not so marked, and the amount of time consumed by the farewell parade, etc., is such a nuisance that all the leading undertakers in this city gladly co-operate with me in urging the closed casket. I have arranged with them that whichever of us reaches the family first after the death should strongly suggest this, and I believe that in all but one case we have been successful. But the moment you get out into the country or even to the smaller cities you find the family usually wishes to leave the casket open, and the ceremony of the closing when the relatives kiss the corpse and dissolve in tears completely destroys the effectiveness of the service as a means of bringing strength and comfort to the bereaved.'

Q. The priest's greeting 'The Lord be with you' between the prayer following the commandments and the collect for the day

(Prayer Book, page 70) seems to me awkward. Why this arrangement? A. This greeting (following historic precedent) introduces a new part of the service. It was put in at the last revision, but it is awkward, and is another example of our badly-planned introductions. One might further ask whether these interspersions of 'Let us pray' really encourage prayer. There is a danger in trying to pray too historically.

Q. Should the congregation kneel when the epistle is read? A. Certainly not. If they kneel at the epistle and stand at the gospel they are paying greater honor to St.Paul than to Christ. Some Roman Catholics kneel, but the Roman Catholic expert, Adrian Fortescue, author of *The Mass, A Study of the Roman Liturgy*, says, 'People hear the epistle, as all lessons except the gospel, sitting.' Let us hope nobody introduces standing. A sermon of the XV century is extant which rebukes certain German nobles because they stood at the epistle to honor St.Paul as being one of their own class!

Q. I have thought for many years that the effect of the Eucharist was often lost in the five-or-more-minute-fuss over the post-communion consumption of the elements. There is nothing impressive to me in the shuttling back and forth of a server between altar and credence table, or in the rustle of a surplice indicating that the priest is cleansing the inside of the cup and platter. Why cannot the cleansing be left until the worshippers have departed? A. Parsons and Jones in *The American Prayer Book* say, 'The ablutions coming after the blessing are a distinct drag on the smooth conclusion of the service.' They also increase the length of the service, which is very undesirable. The priest can easily do the ablutions during the *Gloria in Excelsis* or hymn before the blessing. Is it necessary that congregations rush out in a body at the end of every service? Roman Catholic churches attract many who come to pray before and after the regular services. Bernard Shaw advocates 'going to church' (in an essay by that name) when there is no service. People might respond to the suggestion to remain for a meditation and thanksgiving at the end of every Eucharist.

Q. Is the procession of laymen carrying the offering to the altar wrong? A. This procession of the alms represents the importance of the offering in the old Eucharist, and should be encouraged. The only wrong thing about it is that it inculcates the idea that the layman's chief function in the Church is to handle the money. True but deplorable.

Q. In our parish, boys in scarlet cassocks hold the candles when the priest reads the gospel. Is that wrong? A. Boys are better than nothing. But men are not likely to take their part in services so long as it continues to be a boy's business. The mature laity (not boys) should be encouraged to take part in the Eucharist. Scarlet cassocks are a XIX century abomination.

Q. Why do so many of the clergy read badly? A. (1) American schools do not seem to consider it important to teach children to read. (2) Seminaries do not make good reading a requirement for graduation. (3) Above all—the clergy themselves do not take pains. Most do not think the conduct of services, including good reading, a subject worth serious study. It might awaken the careless if bishops would pick the best reader among the clergy in each diocese, and beg the rest of the clergy to submit themselves to his advice and criticism—above all, criticism.

Q. Should the laity read Morning and Evening Prayer? A. These are essentially lay offices. It is a great pity the clergy so often look on them as their monopoly.

Q. My wife and I both shrink from drinking out of the common communion cup, especially so since reading a warning issued by the Board of Health in our city. Is there any remedy? I understand the General Convention recently debated this subject. I might add that on Easter day, when our rector had no assistant, the administration of the cup kept us in church nearly an extra hour. A. The remedy is simple—leave the communion rail before the cup is offered you. If those who feel as you do (and there are many) would do this, a great reform might come about in a few years without debate or controversy, and no vote of General Convention needed. Before acting it would be courteous, of course, to notify your rector of your intention.

Q. Why does our rector give out the psalms and tell us which page of the Prayer Book to turn to? I have only heard this done in recent years, though in the Prayer Books of my youth the psalm numbers were printed less clearly than they are now. It annoys me. A. You must remember that today there are many of the clergy who conduct their services on the principle of catering to the unintelligent. It is certainly annoying to Church people like ourselves who take pride in the old cultural standards of the Episcopal Church to be treated as if we were children in a kindergarten. But what can we do? We have probably got to grin and bear it. Or else educate the clergy.

Q. Should there be a crucifix on the altar? A. It depends on your theology. If yours is that of the late medieval period, or the pre-scholastic Middle Ages, or the modern Roman Catholic Church, the answer is, yes. If it is that of the New Testament or the ancient Church, which never saw any kind of a crucifix before the time of the crusades, the answer is, no. In my opinion the crucifix carries us too far away from the significance of the original Lord's Supper. But of course one crucifix is better than two, and much better than two crucifixes and several crosses, as we sometimes see them grouped on or around the altar.

Q. I sometimes have to shorten the Communion service. Could I omit the Prayer for the Church? A. Rubrics do not allow any omission, but in any case you must not omit this prayer, which contains two essential features—the intercession, and the solemn offering, the 'sacrifice,' of bread and wine. If you *must* shorten, leave out the commandments, the creed, the Comfortable Words, and of course all trimmings like a 'last gospel'; and put the *Gloria Patri* in place of the *Gloria in Excelsis*.

Q. What would you say to the practice in our Church where the people join with the priest in saying the Prayer of Humble Access and the thanksgiving after communion? A. A novel idea but perhaps a good one in that it makes the service more congregational, and thus gets away from the medieval doctrine that the Holy Communion belongs to the priest and the role of the congregation is that of simple listeners and lookers-on.

Q. Your article 'Profanity in Church' shows a marked lack of Christian charity. Possibly the homiletical masterpieces that you and I and others expound from pulpits as guest preachers are just as obnoxious to our hosts as their service customs are to us. Why give freedom to your prejudices in your column rather than providing facts? A. I agree that many of us do preach pretty bad, perhaps even 'obnoxious,' sermons, though I doubt if our sermons are, generally speaking, as bad as our services. But why is it uncharitable to criticize both services and sermons? Lawyers have to win their cases in court in the face of aggressive criticism. The misfortune of the clergy is that they have to plead only before uncritical, not to say submissive, congregations. Thus they fall under the lure of a self-satisfaction that carries them on from bad to worse. Their best friends are their friendly critics, and if they had more such friends they might improve both services and sermons to the point of winning back some of the discerning lay people who now simply stay away from their churches.

Q. Is there a better way of administering confirmation than for the bishop to pass from one to another along the communion rail? A. One hesitates to advise bishops, but from the point of view of the congregation it seems much more dignified and interesting for the bishop to sit in the middle before the altar, and confirm the kneeling candidates as they present themselves to him one by one, or two by two.

Q. Where can I learn more about the liturgical movement? A. The *Orate Fratres*, a monthly magazine published by the Benedictine monks at Collegeville, Minnesota, is an excellent exponent of this movement in the Roman Catholic Church. *The Parish*

Communion, edited by Father Hebert, is a good Anglican book of a somewhat pro-Roman character.

Q. Why is there no Advent preface? A. Because of the timidity of our Prayer Book revisers who felt bound by medieval precedent. An Advent preface would be eminently proper and edifying.

Q. Is it desirable that the person who administers the chalice should wipe it each time he hands it to a new communicant? A. It is very undesirable. It simply calls attention to germs which are probably not there, and which, if they were, would not be eliminated by the 'purificator.' It would not be necessary to criticize this unpleasant custom if we had communion in one kind.

Q. In the 'Eucharist Simplified' I find the suggestion that the following form be used in place of the blessing: 'And now let each one hasten to do good works, to please God and live aright, devoting himself to the Church, practising the things he has learned, advancing in the service of God.' Is not this an abrupt way to end the Communion service? Is there any authority for it? A. The older forms of the Eucharist were composed on the assumption that the Communion itself, the reception of the body and blood of Christ, was the real blessing for which the faithful had come together. So the service ended immediately after the Communion. The original ending of the Roman Mass was '*Ite missa est*'—'Go, it is the dismissal.' All after that is later accretion. The blessing never found its way into English missals. The formula reprinted in the 'Eucharist Simplified' is from the *Apostolic Tradition* of Hippolytus, a recently discovered document published in an English translation by Dr. Easton of the General Theological Seminary. It was compiled about 217 by Hippolytus, a presbyter or bishop of the Church in Rome, but it may preserve the liturgical forms of 180 or even earlier.

Q. One parson writes about the recommendation of communion in one kind: 'I cannot think of anything more silly, more impolite, or more unrubrical. To reduce the matter to something of an absurdity: Question—"I am invited to the White House for dinner; I am afraid the dessert will make me ill; what shall I do?" To which Dorothy Dix makes reply: "The remedy is simple—leave the table before the dessert is offered you." Could anything cause more confusion, or be more absurd, than the hasty withdrawal of a goodly number of guests from the table before the offending pudding should appear? To return the discussion, reverently, to the matter of the Lord's Table, it would seem that any solution to the problem would be preferable to the one suggested. If the communicant remains at the communion rail it at least gives the priest the opportunity to do what the rubric definitely orders to do—"deliver the same to the people . . . into their hands." If the communicant chooses to receive the chalice and return it to the priest untouched by his lips, that is his own responsibility. He at least has not been openly discourteous. There is the alternative, also, of dipping the consecrated wafer into the chalice when it is passed to him. There is also the regular and usual method of drinking from the chalice as every priest of the Church drinks from it each Sunday—in many parishes more often—without any harmful effects, so far as I have been able to learn.' A. If anyone thinks it more courteous or rubrical to receive the chalice and return it, by all means let him do it that way. As to drinking out of the common cup, the following communication from a lady who belongs to an altar guild is to the point: 'In washing purificators it is a great sacrilege to me to find them deeply colored with lip-stick and paint. Must I drink paint put into the sacred wine by my neighbor? It is high time the Church took a stand.'

Q. Several have strongly advocated giving out the page of the psalter, especially as a help to strangers. Here, e.g. is one comment: 'Many who attend our services are only "unintelligent" in that they have had no training in the technicalities of the Prayer Book services, and they are most appreciative of a little courtesy in the matter of guidance shown either by clergyman or neighbor in the pew. During the years of my ministry in California and other parts of the West I have been thanked repeatedly by visitors, and also by a considerable number of somewhat lax "choice souls" of our own communion, for the help afforded by the occasional announcement of the proper page. I know at least two bishops who highly commend the practice, and I sincerely hope the Dean will "educate the clergy" in this direction, instead of the other, when he realizes the error of his ways.' A. This critic seems to forget that if he announces the page he thereby deprives the neighbor in the pew of the opportunity to show this 'little courtesy' to strangers. Is it really desirable that the clergy do everything themselves, and leave little or nothing to the man or woman in the pew? And must worship always be made pleasant and easy? Might it not be a good thing for the stranger to find that he had something to learn in order to qualify as a worshipper?

X. APPENDIX

THE NEXT 150 YEARS

WE MAY well be proud of the record our Book of Common Prayer has made in the last one hundred and fifty years. In its very beginning it brought Seabury, the High Churchman, and White, the Low Churchman, together, and ever since then it has served as a bond of unity between all sections of the Church. In some of its features, notably its Prayer of Consecration, it has given the lead to other branches of the Anglican communion. It has stimulated in American Roman Catholics the desire for a liturgy in the vernacular. It has had an enormous influence on the worship of all the Protestant denominations.

A consideration of the notable services the American Book of Common Prayer has rendered since its adoption on October 16, 1789, to all sections of the Christian Church may well make us hopeful of what it may accomplish in the next one hundred and fifty years. What that may be no one can forecast. Everything depends on the Church, and for the moment on ourselves. But anyone can hope. And it may not be amiss for an individual to try to forecast the lines along which he hopes the Church and the Prayer Book will move.

Any rational hope must rest on a careful scrutiny and analysis of the existing attitude toward worship in the Christian world. And to even the most superficial observer it must be evident that all the Churches are today being swept along in what may be described in general terms as a 'liturgical movement.' We have been accustomed to think of the Roman Church as immovable, but the title, 'liturgical movement,' belongs in a special sense to that Church. In the past twenty-five years a slow but very significant revolution has been taking place. There has come a new understanding of the whole historical development of the liturgy. It is now frankly admitted by many Roman scholars that not a few of the generally accepted formulations of eucharistic doctrine, such as those relating to the sacrifice of the Mass and the priesthood of the laity, are exaggerated statements which grew out of the bitter theological controversies of the XVI and XVII centuries, and which should be discarded or greatly modified today. There has been a growing recognition of the fact that many features of the present Mass are medieval accretions which exhibit the liturgical deterioration characteristic of the period out of which they came. There is a demand for a return to primitive standards, to the New Testament, and the Fathers, similar to that which our own Anglican divines attempted in the Reformation period. And the interesting thing is that this scientific, reasonable, liberal approach to liturgical problems has had no official discouragement— quite the contrary—and is slowly permeating the whole Roman body.

As to the Protestant groups, everyone is familiar with the fact that for many years they have been borrowing prayers from the Prayer Book, organizing surpliced choirs, building churches with altars, and decorating altars with crosses and candles. But the Protestant liturgical movement goes much deeper than that. For example, leading Presbyterian theologians both in Scotland and this country are teaching eucharistic doctrine which cannot be described as other than essentially Catholic. The United Church of Canada has adopted a Prayer Book which approaches Catholic tradition far nearer than anything that would have been possible in any Protestant denomination a generation ago. American Lutherans are deploring the fact that their services have been far too much colored by XVIII century pietism, and are calling for a return to the orthodox standards of the earlier Lutheranism. Their Common Service Book, frankly indebted to our Prayer Book, has Catholic features which are lacking in our own book. These examples taken at random will suggest other developments which will have come under the notice of every reader.

In this situation our own Church, with an incomparable Prayer Book, and holding its generally-recognized mediating, reconciling, and strategic position, stands facing a great opportunity. We can enter intelligently and whole-heartedly into this liturgical movement. And in doing this we can not only enrich and deepen our own devotion, but we can make our Prayer Book a standard and ideal to which other churches will turn for light and leading. I venture the following ten suggestions as to how we might perfect our Prayer Book. They deal only with the Holy Eucharist, but that is, of course, the heart of the whole liturgical problem.

1. We must cut loose from the XVI century English political tradition which makes of every sentence of the Communion service a fixed, sacrosanct, inalterable entity, to depart from which is to break the law and to expose our congregations to heresy, schism, privy conspiracy, and rebellion. We will of course preserve and cherish Catholic tradition. But we must at the same time interpret rubrics liberally, and keep an open mind to revise, to enrich, to simplify, and to adapt the Communion service to the needs of our own day, remembering that such procedure is itself a part of the Catholic tradition. After all, as St.Thomas says, the purpose of sacraments is to help man in his spiritual life.

2. We must keep the goal always in mind—which is to make the Holy Eucharist the chief service on every Sunday in every parish. We shall reach that goal most surely, I venture to think, not by returning to the Middle Ages and copying Roman methods, but by going forward, gradually, to a real parish communion.

3. The service should be made simpler and more intelligible. The Communion service of even the first Prayer Book of Edward VI was easier for the plain man to follow than our own. The great Roman Catholic scholar, Edmund Bishop, describing the Roman rite of the IV century, says it was 'simple, practical, clear, brief.' That is what ours ought to be if we are going to popularize the

eucharistic message and allow it to work for the greatest good to the greatest number.

4. Repetitions should be eliminated, e.g. in the Prayer of Consecration. And shortening, e.g. by the omission of the confession, absolution, and Comfortable Words, should be allowed, something which could usually be done by a simple change in the rubrics from 'shall' to 'may.'

5. The calendar should be revised. Why keep a festival of St. Bartholomew, whose only claim is that his name appears in the New Testament list of apostles, and omit saints like St.Augustine and St.Francis, who have a real message for our day?

6. There should be a revised lectionary. Our present selection of epistles and gospels is to a large extent accidental and arbitrary. With the help of modern Biblical scholarship it would be easily possible to make a wiser selection. And if the Eucharist is not to be preceded by Matins (as the first revisers expected) there should be a provision for Old Testament lessons. The Roman Mass has a much better selection of Scripture readings than ours, but there are Roman scholars who have argued for radical omissions and additions in their traditional Sunday lectionary, which is similar to ours. For all Churchmen familiar with our present epistles and gospels any change would be, of course, a sacrifice of precious, sentimental associations. But the gain in the long run would be great.

7. A place should be made for the psalms—introits, graduals, etc. And there might be some recognition of the traditional music of the Mass.

8. The offering should be separated from the Prayer for the Church.

9. Intercession has always been a great feature of the Eucharist. But our stately XVI century Prayer for the Church is so unsatisfactory that some of the unliturgically minded clergy are actually shortening the service by leaving it out. Its phraseology is antiquated—e.g. 'all Christian rulers' (i.e. kings), 'punishment of wickedness and vice,' 'lively word,' 'comfort and succor'; and in

general it lacks the simplicity and directness intercession should have. Furthermore, it omits all reference to city, state, and nation, to popular sovereignty, parish and family, foreign and domestic missions, peace, social justice, Christian education, and other matters for which congregations want, or should want, to pray.

10. The long wait during communion—which will become more burdensome if parish communions increase—is one of the greatest drawbacks to eucharistic devotion. The simple remedy is communion in one kind. This need not involve any revision or legislation. The laity can be encouraged to return to their seats before the cup is administered. This leaves everybody free to follow his own convictions. The western medieval Church made this important change in the XIII century without any clamor or controversy. The same ought to be possible for us.

To conclude: The Holy Eucharist is essentially the 'sacrament of unity,' as great theologians like St.Augustine, St.Thomas, and John Calvin have always taught. But to make it the sacrament of unity requires a faith sufficient to go beyond words and formulas, beyond national and ecclesiastical habits. Ours is the responsibility and the duty to make the most of our Prayer Book Eucharist as a living, spiritual tradition. Thus it would attract far-flung and unsuspected loyalties, and the next one hundred and fifty years might witness its development into an increasingly effective instrument for the promotion of unity among all the churches of our sadly divided and distracted Christendom. May it not be the special vocation of our Church to make that contribution to the fulfilment of our Lord's great eucharistic petition 'that they all may be one'?

RELIGION, MUSIC, AND LITURGY*

WHAT music is fitted to that essentially corporate form of worship, the traditional worship of the historical, visible, Christian Church as it is embodied in the great primitive liturgies?

I suggest that those liturgies gather up adoration, offering, and

* Adapted from a paper read before the American Theological Society.

communion, and that every satisfactory form of worship should gather them up, in an act which is essentially of the nature of drama. In order to commend this idea as without theological *parti pris* I shall take an illustration from modern Communism. Last fall, so I have been told, a meeting was held in Symphony Hall, Boston, in the interest of the Community Chest. The meeting was well advertised and there were eminent and eloquent speakers appealing on behalf of this worthy object. But the hall was only half full. That same night in the same city a Communist rally was going on in a much larger hall, and the hall was packed to overflowing with shouting, enthusiastic participants. How account for this phenomenon? Not surely that all the citizens of Boston including the Communists did not wish large sums to go to the Community Chest. Such money would go to those burdened with poverty and disease, to the hungry, helpless, and dying, go to meet needs familiar to all, and possessing a universal and urgent human appeal. Indeed the very words community and communism suggest the fundamental identity of purpose of the two meetings. But the crowd went to the skating rink. Why? Because they saw poverty and wealth on the stage as contestants in a momentous and exciting drama, the world revolution, and they felt that in this millennial drama they were themselves participating by their presence.

In the summer of 1936 I joined a crowd of thousands of Communists packed into the largest theatre in Paris. The play presented was Romain Rolland's *Quatorze Juillet*. A dozen years ago the play was put on the Paris stage and it fell flat, but 1936 was the opportune moment. The stirring events which led up to the fall of the Bastille on 14 July 1789 had become symbols of the class struggle of July 1936. There on the stage could be seen the communion of the revolutionary saints like Camille Desmoulins (of whom the world was not worthy) putting us to shame for our inactivity, yet calling to us to carry on the good fight for *liberté, égalité, fraternité*. As the historic scenes and speeches symbolized and expressed our emotions we were led up to the culminating moment when in silence we stood for a moment to remember our suffering brothers in Spain, and then the *Internationale* was sung accompanied by the uplifted hand and the clenched first of the Communist salute. It was all so stirring that I went twice to this Communist mass.

My conviction is that we have got to make the Christian religion more dramatic, or our churches will gradually empty while the skating rinks and theatres are filling up with more and more Communists. This will be a hard thing to do until we have a clean-cut theology, some such theology as the Church always had up to the Reformation. But I suggest that one step in the right direction would be to restore its dramatic character to Christian worship, and to accomplish that end by putting back the Holy Eucharist into the place which it always occupied until the Reformation, as the chief act of congregational worship on every Lord's day.

This may seem to you to be a Romanist or an Anglo-Catholic proposal in disguise, but I am not, as a matter of fact, appealing for the Roman Mass. That service, as is well known, is a very degenerate liturgical form, full of interpolations and confusions of thought. Nor am I trying to commend to you the Communion service of the Book of Common Prayer, which in its Scottish and American form is certainly better than the medieval Mass, but is far too much the chance product of the clashing medievalism and Calvinism of the XVI century. The service we seem to me to need for our Sunday morning congregations is a combination of the primitive and the modern, and my conviction is that the general introduction of such a service would be the greatest move we could possibly make in the direction of church unity, and my personal opinion is that a conference on such a subject would have a much greater result than anything that is likely to come out of either Edinburgh or Oxford: at any rate it seems to me clear that the idea ought to make a convincing appeal to every genuine Protestant. For this I suggest three reasons.

1. The first Protestants did not intentionally revolutionize the traditional worship of the Church. Indeed the Eucharist continued as the chief Sunday morning service in Lutheran churches until the XVIII century, and in part so continues today. It was the epigoni of the Reformation who failed to preserve this most ancient and Christian tradition which for so many centuries had united both orthodox and heretic, catholic and schismatic, and who dethroned the Eucharist from its age-long position as the center of the Church's devotional life.

2. The appeal of the Protestant reformers was to primitive Christianity. The fact that in the matter of worship they knew so little what the ancient liturgical tradition was, and the fact that they were themselves so obsessed with medievalism that they could not appreciate the primitive tradition ought not, it would seem, to prevent the Protestants of today from carrying out what was undoubtedly their fundamental purpose—to go back to that primitive tradition, to learn from it, and perhaps to re-establish their continuity with it.

3. The ancient liturgies had many features supposed to be dear to Protestants. Without entering into detail I may mention:

a. The important place given in those liturgies to the Holy Scriptures of both the Old and New Testaments with a special emphasis upon the reading of the gospel which was carried out with impressive ceremonial;

b. The important part taken by the congregation—this was before the medieval cleavage between clergy and laity;

c. The emphasis on fellowship; witness the *fractio panis* of the *Capella Graeca*, and the kiss of peace, an essential part of so many of the liturgies;

d. The simple but fundamental theology, no splitting hairs over transubstantiation, consubstantiation, etc.;

e. The close connection made between prayer and conduct, the Eucharist a part of the disciplinary system.

f. Another point. The exaltation of sacrament and symbol is

not so obviously Protestant. Yet the Protestant did not need to wait for Hitler to teach him how indispensable sacraments are to mass control, for Luther had already said 'word *and* sacraments'; and he need not study the philosophy of Ernst Cassirer to discover the important place of symbolic form in human life, for J.S.Bach, perhaps the greatest creative genius of all Protestantism, had expressed his Christian faith in symbolic music.

So much for liturgy. Now what is the appropriate liturgical music? It should be directed Godwards. It should be intrinsically good; it should avoid the aesthetically crude and the shallow and sentimental, what corresponds to Plato's Phrygian mode. It should be subordinated to the service: it should be congregational, and of the kind to appeal to the young and the intelligent young.

It should be simple and austere. I say this with a sense of shame at being an Episcopalian rather than a Presbyterian. Last Christmas morning I started out to go to an Episcopalian service. As I approached the church and heard the strains of the Communion service sung in that most approved D'Oyly Carte style, so popular in our Episcopal churches today, my heart sank. But fortunately I had made a mistake in the time, the service was already half over, and I withdrew to a Congregational church near by, where the Communion service had not yet begun. That service, simple, austere, not overloaded with music, devoutly rendered, was a memorable and real Holy Communion.

My feeling about this D'Oyly Carte church music is that the choirs and congregations, conscious that they do not know much or believe much, are trying to cover up their uncertain faith by singing orthodox hymns at the highest attainable pressure. They are afraid to drop out of the major key for fear that the bottom will drop out of their religion. They put vocal mechanism and vociferous self-expression in place of that humble and contrite spirit which should subdue the worshipper in the presence of God.

Finally, we should draw on all the resources of our traditional

Christian musical heritage, and especially should we extend our hospitality to medieval plainsong, though of course the historical should not be pushed to the point of becoming archeological. There is no doubt a widespread aversion to plainsong, but here I would like to quote Professor Archibald Davison, who, so far as I can see, is right in making the point that many modern musicians have come to dislike the rigidity and arbitrariness of the major and minor systems, and are going back to the free modes of the Middle Ages. If this is true in the field of secular music, it seems to me likely that plainsong will increasingly attract and satisfy the more adventurous of the rising generation. Again, plainsong does seem to me to express just that principle of transcendence which belongs to the best pictorial art of our time, a principle which is an essential part of the Christian religion. And it strikes that note of unsatisfied aspiration which should characterize all Christian worshippers.

THE HISTORY OF THE LITURGICAL MOVEMENT

THE CELEBRATION of our own 150th Prayer Book anniversary would seem a fitting time at which to survey the growth of the liturgical movement in the Roman Catholic Church, for there is no doubt that this is one of the most interesting religious developments of our time. It has not gone very far in this country, nor has it made any great progress in any country among the rank and file of the clergy and laity. To a great extent it is a movement which belongs to scholars and theologians. It is thus a continuation of the important contribution made by members of the Roman Church since the Reformation to the understanding of its historic liturgy.

This contribution has been largely the work of the monastic orders. In the XVII and XVIII centuries the center of liturgiology was the great Benedictine Congregation of St.Maur, with its mother house in Paris, which edited the well-known Benedictine editions of the Fathers. Mabillon (+1707), a member of this Congregation, first published the famous *Ordines Romani*, which record the ceremonial of the Mass from the first *Ordo* of about 700. Edmund Martène (+1739), a member of the Congregation, produced the *De Antiquis Ecclesiae Ritibus*, a work of lasting value, partly because it gives an account of liturgical documents since lost. Among the French Oratorians of this time were Pierre LeBrun (+1729), perhaps the greatest of all liturgical scholars, and Eusèbe Renaudot (+1720) who, with LeBrun, investigated the Oriental liturgies and demonstrated the place of the invocation in the Eucharist, somewhat as the English and Scottish Nonjurors did in the same period. In the XIX century one of the best known liturgiologists was Dom Prosper Guéranger (+1875), who desired to revive the Maurist Congregation, which had been suppressed at the time of the French Revolution, but was forbidden to do so by the pope. He then founded the monastery at Solesmes which became the center for the revival of the Gregorian chant. Among other well-known Roman Catholic liturgical scholars in France in the XIX century have been Delisle, Cagin, Andrieu, Duchesne, and Cabrol; in Germany, Ebner, Dreves, and Casel; in Belgium, Callewaert and Morin; in England, Edmund Bishop.

The modern liturgical movement may be said to date from the period following the Great War, and its development from the first has been largely under the leadership of the Benedictine monks of Maria Laach, near the Rhine in Germany, which traces its inspiration back through Beuron in Bavaria to Solesmes. The influence of this monastery has been very great, not only in the field of scholarship but in the spiritual life of the German Roman Catholic Church. Competent observers have said that that church could hardly have withstood the Nazi persecution as it has done had it not been for the leadership of Maria Laach. The movement is strong in Belgium, where in its inception it had the patronage of Cardinal Mercier. It is well established in Rome; some, in fact, look on the *Moto Proprio* of Pius X on church music, issued in

1910, as a landmark in the history of the movement. On this continent it is favored by the present Archbishop of Quebec, and at Collegeville, Minnesota, a Benedictine monastery is furthering the movement by issuing much popular liturgical literature, including a valuable magazine, *Orate Fratres*.

The essence of the movement is a return to primitive standards of worship. This means a decided repudiation of the degenerate eucharistic doctrine and ceremonial which prevailed in the late Middle Ages and which continued in an exaggerated form in the Roman Church of the Counter-Reformation period. It means a protest against the rigid liturgical uniformity so successfully advocated by Dom Guéranger at the time of Pius IX, the result of which was the suppression of ancient local usages such as those of the Lyons diocese— 'a lamentable result of ignorance and bad will,' to quote the words of the distinguished Roman scholar Dom Morin. It means the repudiation of what a Roman bishop has recently called 'that falsely sentimental and superstitious piety which constitutes a grave spiritual malady in our own times.'

The Mass in spite of its many defects has preserved some of the best features of the ancient liturgies. Thus 'Back to the mass!' which is one of the watch-words of the movement, means a restoration of congregational worship; for the Mass is not a service to be said by the priest *for* the people (the medieval idea), but is the prayer of the whole congregation—'*we* pray and beseech thee, *we* offer, let *us* give thanks,' etc. It means a return to the emphasis on offering rather than the medieval emphasis on presence and adoration. Cardinal Faulhaber has revived the primitive offertory procession in which the people bring their bread, wine, and other food to the altar, a timely move in face of the Nazi opposition to all the charitable enterprises of the church. There is a return to the old custom, still found in the Roman basilicas, of the priest standing behind the altar facing the people as he celebrates mass. Churches have been built with an altar in the center, around which the people gather, that they may see and understand what goes on at the altar and join intimately with the priest in the successive parts of the liturgy. In many churches there is a 'dialogue mass' in which the people take their part in the Latin responses. Every attempt is made to surmount the difficulty of worshipping in an unknown tongue. Sometimes a second priest repeats whole sections in the vernacular for the benefit of the congregation. People's missals, with Latin on one side and the language of the country on the other, have been issued in enormous quantities. All this tends to emphasize the fact that in the Mass the laity exercise their priesthood. And there is a reformulation of the whole doctrine of the sacrifice of the Mass.

How far these ideas have penetrated even the English Roman Catholic body may be judged by two quotations taken at random from recent numbers of the *Dublin Review*. One contributor speaks of 'the ignorant superstition not merely that the Latin Church is the Catholic Church, but that there is something essentially superior about the Latin rite and those who have the privilege of using it.' (What a shock to our fellow churchmen who have been for so many years trying to persuade us of the essential superiority of the Latin rite!) Another refers to 'the popular illusion that the mass is simply a means of procuring the sacramental presence of our Lord in order that we may receive him in Communion.' In the Mass, he says, 'the oblational must predominate over the adorational.'

It is apparent that the ideals of the Roman liturgical movement are similar to those that animated Cranmer and the other reformers in their preparation of the English Book of Common Prayer. They too were liturgical scholars. The honorable tradition of liturgical scholarship begun by Cranmer and continued by the Caroline divines and the Non-jurors still survives. We may well be proud of the contributions made to liturgical study and indeed to the liturgical movement by our own Church in modern times. Important publications of original documents have issued from the Henry Bradshaw Society and the Alcuin Club. The names of

Frere, Brightman, Wilson, Feltoe, W.C.Bishop, Wickham Legg, Percy Dearmer, to mention only a few, are well known. And the publication of Dr. Easton's *Apostolic Tradition of Hippolytus,* Parsons and Jones' *American Prayer Book,* and Dr. Cirlot's *Early Eucharist* is a good omen of the revival of liturgical study among ourselves.

But the Oxford Movement bequeathed to us an evil heritage. Instead of building on the fine liturgical tradition of the Non-jurors, which had been so successfully popularized by John Wesley, its leaders turned with longing eyes toward Rome. To a serious degree they were mere copyists and sentimentalists. We can today make a sober estimate of their achievement in the architectural field. We see them roving about England, desecrating its cathedrals and parish churches, spending vast sums on 'restoration' and replacing the old by their childish make-believe Gothic. Such ideas carried into the liturgical field produced the 'ritualists' who tore down Anglican tradition and copied all the wrong things. They replaced the parish communion by high and low mass. They imposed vulgar ceremonial on long-suffering congregations just because it had been pronounced 'correct' by the papal Congregation of Rites. They pursued the same ultramontane ideal of uniformity which Dom Guéranger had inflicted on the continental church. They ignored the fact that their beloved Roman ceremonial came out of the period which Father Gregory Dix has described as one of 'unexampled liturgical decay,' and they spread the cultus of many forms and ceremonies which are anathema to learned and orthodox leaders of the Roman liturgical movement today.

At the present time there is a considerable liturgical movement in the Church of England, led by Father Hebert of the Society of the Sacred Mission, author of *Liturgy and Society.* Its weakness is that it is the outgrowth of 'ritualism.' Its leaders have been so long travelling on the pro-Roman road that they find it difficult to turn about. They undervalue Anglican tradition, and they are so devoted to their 'Western use' that they find it hard to face realities. An illustration is furnished by Father Hebert in his really valuable book entitled *Parish Communion*. He makes an eloquent plea for a Sunday morning communion at which the whole parish shall communicate—by which he means all who come fasting! 'Some of the Anglo-Catholic clergy are,' he admits, 'more rigid than the Roman Church, but we must uphold fasting communion as a rule.' Those who have to eat before the parish communion are to get a dispensation from the parish priest! It is hard to suppose that many of the intelligent laity will accept this advice, or that many of the clergy will desire thus to sit in grave judgment on the dietary habits of docile parishioners.

Nothing is more important than that the liturgical movement should take the right direction in this country at the present time. It ought not to be left to the guidance of those clergy who dare do nothing without Roman sanction. Evangelically-minded churchmen are faced with a great opportunity. By carrying the Prayer Book reform inaugurated at the Reformation a step further forward, and by adapting our inherited forms of worship to the modern situation, they can prepare the Church to meet the needs of a generation it has done so much to mislead and to alienate.

WHY BISHOPS?

THIS QUESTION is often asked of Episcopalians, and every well-informed member of the Episcopal Church ought to be able to say not only why his Church has bishops, but why bishops are so important that they give their name to the Church—for an Episcopal Church means a Church with an episcopate, i.e. a Church which is organized under bishops.

A short and practical answer might be this—we have bishops because everywhere and always anything to be well done has to be done by an organized group under the right leadership. But this answer leads to two further questions: (1) Is organization desirable in religion? (2) Do bishops give the right leadership? Let us take these questions in order.

Organization, it is true, is often a nuisance, especially in this commercial age which is so much given to efficiency; and the organization of religion is often both unlovely and ineffective. One can understand how some people say that the best interests of religion require that everybody should be free to serve God in his own way without the intrusion of any church rule, doctrine, or ceremony, or who say they believe in Christ but not in the Church or in the churches. Certainly freedom is a part of the Christian ideal. Certainly the churches never adequately represent Christ. But are we therefore to discard all church organization?

This emphasis on individualism and this hostility to organized religion came in, as is well known, with the Protestant Reformation in the XVI century. At that time the Church in western Europe, the one Church which had come down from the beginning and claimed to speak with divine authority, had in many ways discredited itself. Weighed down with the accumulated mistakes of centuries, it badly needed reform. It had amassed extensive wealth and was using it for the benefit of the favored few. Under the domination of the Bishop of Rome it kept the laity in subjection to the clergy, and emphasized outward ceremonial conformity at the expense of the inward spirit and of Christian conduct. Protests began long before the XVI century. The final and violent break came where abuses were at their worst, as in Bohemia, North Germany, and Scotland, under the leadership of Hus, Luther, and John Knox.

The reformers appealed to the New Testament and the early Church Fathers. In these writings they found a Church with no accumulated wealth, no fixed traditions, no elaborate ceremonial, no cathedrals, no canon law, no monks, no pope. They undertook to bring back such a Church to their own time. Their sincerity was praiseworthy, but their attempt was bound to fail. First, because it is never possible to 'turn back the clock' in historical development. Second, the reformers had not sufficient historical knowledge to understand the Church of the first centuries. Third, they fell into such violent controversy with the pope and with each other that their judgment became warped. Fourth, while many of them appreciated the importance which the New Testament and the early Fathers attached to the unity of the Church, and wanted only reform, others said the old Church was too corrupt to be reformed, and started new churches according to their own ideas. Fifth, the emphasis laid on personal salvation and the claim of each individual to interpret the Bible for himself added to the general confusion. The final result was as far as possible from the New Testament ideal.

The simple fact is that individualism does not work in the sphere of religion or anywhere else in life. No man liveth to himself. Man is a social being. Organization means co-operation, fellowship, brotherhood, love. Church organization is thus not a mere human device; it is a divine thing.

And that is the New Testament point of view. While it gives the completest possible recognition to the individual, his rights, and responsibilities, it relates the individual to the corporate life. It bids men save their souls, but it tells them to do it in saving others and along with others. In the New Testament the organization of the Church is not a matter of indifference, or expediency, or individual caprice. The Church is the body of Christ! It is the true Israel, the successor of the Jewish Church. It is the Kingdom of God in the making. Its members are bound together by sacraments. Its mission is to go into all the world and secure new members. It is the Church of the Living God, the pillar and ground of the truth.

That is the Church in which Episcopalians believe, the one Church which has reached across the ages to our own times and is here today. Though sadly divided, it is the Church for which our Lord prayed 'that they all may be one.' It is the one Holy, Catholic, Apostolic Church of which the creeds speak.

We come now to the question of leadership. And first we must recognize that leadership as well as organization is a divine and necessary thing. Every social group must have leadership, and on the quality of that leadership its effectiveness and its very life depend. This is a principle which we all recognize in politics, in education, in business. More and more in these days the tendency grows to put responsibility on leaders, be they presidents, premiers, or highly paid business executives.

And Christianity is a religion of leadership. The great leader is Jesus Christ. He trained the apostles to be leaders, and sent them forth to preach the gospel. Just how this leadership passed from the apostles to the bishops is, as a matter of historical knowledge, not altogether clear, but in the beginning of the II century we find Ignatius the martyr Bishop of Antioch, using such phrases as this: 'Do nothing apart from the bishop.' And a century and a half later Cyprian of Carthage, another martyr bishop, writes: 'If anyone is not with the bishop he is not in the Church.' These quotations are typical of the early Church, and from that time to the Reformation in all branches of the Church, European, Asian, and African, leadership was recognized as belonging to the bishops, the successors of the apostles. Thus Episcopalians feel that the historic episcopate unites them to Christ, to the New Testament Church, and to the Church of all ages and lands.

It must of course be frankly admitted that the bishops have not always been good leaders. This was obviously true in the late Middle Ages when the Bishops of Rome assumed so much authority and made so many mistakes. And it has been true of many other periods, notably of the XVIII century in England, where the bishops were a worldly-minded lot, and by their unsympathetic treatment of John Wesley created the unfortunate division which still exists between Methodists and Episcopalians.

It is fair to ask whether in an Episcopal Church this sort of hard-hearted officialism and abuse of power may not be always expected. The answer is that as a historical fact such unfortunate developments have almost always come from an alliance of the Church with the State (as in XVIII century England) or the transformation of the Church into a sort of state (as was the case in the Middle Ages) and bishops have been chosen for other reasons than their apostolic character. To us in democratic America such a development seems no longer possible. So long as the separation of Church and State endures, bishops can be freely chosen by the Church and free to serve its interests.

Such was, in fact, the episcopacy of the primitive Church. The bishop was elected by popular vote. Far from being an arbitrary ruler he was in the fullest sense the representative of the whole congregation or diocese. He was the instrument of the Spirit-bearing body. He ruled in the name of the Church, and his authority was that of the Church itself.

To sum up, Episcopalians hold to the following convictions: (1) Religion is fundamentally social as well as individual. (2) The Christian religion was from the beginning embodied in the one Church, Holy, Catholic, and Apostolic. (3) The Church has since the days of the apostles been governed by bishops, and in spite of manifold lapses—for the Church is human as well as divine—the episcopal form of government has throughout the ages enjoyed the divine presence and favor. Most Episcopalians would say episcopacy belongs to the *esse* (the very being) of the Church; all would agree that it belongs to its *bene esse* (well being). (4) The historic episcopate binds us not only to the Church of the past but to the Roman Catholic and Orthodox Eastern Churches of today. (5) Episcopacy is not only historic and traditional, it is modern and adaptable, it combines law and order with freedom and development; it is well fitted to give effective leadership to the Church in the face of modern problems and difficulties. (6) The American Episcopal Church believes that the historic episcopate offers a promising basis of unity for our separated American Christianity, and it hopes and prays that this unity will ultimately embrace Christians of whatever name everywhere in the world.

Is Theological Education Important?

Theology is the science of God, and it was once considered the 'queen of the sciences.' Today, however, it is a dethroned queen, stripped of its one-time privilege and influence. Why is this? Obviously no Christian can think of a science which leads to the knowledge of God as unimportant. But the typical modern man, even the modern Christian, is inclined to question how much theology can help him to know God. He remembers that theologians have in the past made many mistakes. And perhaps for that reason he often prefers to think things out for himself, and to trust his own instinct, with the help of a good life, and perhaps an occasional prayer. It is more than probable, however, that he knows little or nothing about what theology is, or how it is studied and taught in a modern theological seminary.

What then is theology? We begin with the Bible, which, as the Prayer Book tells us, contains all things necessary to salvation. The layman can, of course, learn much about God by simply reading the Bible, and drawing his own conclusions. But experience proves that this method has its serious drawbacks. Again and again across the centuries have Christians, and even great bodies of Christians, found justification in the Bible for the most erroneous and even immoral ideas. The student of the Bible needs more than sincerity and zeal. He needs knowledge. The Bible is a world in itself. It is not one book, but many, written at widely separated times and under very diverse circumstances. A knowledge of this cultural and historical background is essential for an understanding of the Bible. In the past hundred years such knowledge has enormously increased. The Bible has thus become almost a new book, and one vastly more intelligible, more real, more instructive, and more helpful. Biblical science, then, the old Scriptures from the modern point of view, must be an important department in every theological seminary.

Again, God is revealed not only in the Bible but in all Christian history. Our theology would be one-sided if we took no account of what the wise and devout have in past ages thought about God, and how Christians before our time have tried to live the Christian life as members of a Christian society. That is Church History—an important section of theology. Then there is Christian Ethics. To be a good Christian it is not enough simply to want to do right. Mistakes in the field of conduct, even if well-meant, discredit religion and harm others as well as ourselves. It is the part of Christian Ethics to describe and define the Christian way of life, taking account at the same time of other ethical systems, both ancient and modern. Finally, there is Theology in the narrow sense—sometimes called Systematic or Dogmatic Theology. It brings Bible study, Church History, and Christian Ethics into a unified system; it generalizes from the conclusions reached in those other fields, and it endeavors to relate theological science with all other sciences of whatever kind. It deals with such fundamental problems as sin and salvation, the nature of man, creation and redemption, time and eternity, the problem of evil.

Suppose the Church had no theology. We Christians would then be forced to look for exact knowledge to the natural sciences. It would in that case mean little to be a Christian or to belong to a Church, for a religion that does not offer trustworthy knowledge about the problems of life must be a very unsatisfactory religion. And may it not be just because modern man has pushed theology so much to one side, and pinned his faith so much to the natural sciences, and accepted their interpretations of life, that the present world chaos, the general collapse of humanitarian ideals both among men and nations, the might-makes-right philosophy, the falsehood, cruelty, and tyranny, have come upon the world as they have?

Realizing the importance of a learned, living, rational theology, the Church has established its theological seminaries. The professors on their faculties are giving their lives to the study of theology, and seek to become experts in their various fields. By writing and teaching they are helping the Church, both the clergy and the laity, to think clearly about the Christian revelation and the fundamental doctrines of the Church. And just as medical science is closely bound up with the efficiency of the medical schools, so is theological science greatly dependent upon our theological seminaries, and theology is likely to flourish in proportion as our theological faculties are competent and our theological seminaries are adequately equipped.

But the chief immediate task of the theological seminaries is to train students for the Church's ministry. Such students need to learn the fundamentals of Christian theology as already outlined. They should study under teachers as competent as those who are preparing the future lawyers and doctors in the law and medical schools. And, beside that, they need to be trained to become teachers themselves. They must learn how to make their knowledge available and acceptable to others, they must learn how to preach, how to conduct the services of the Church, how to carry on the many practical activities which the Church expects of its priests and pastors.

And, finally, what is perhaps more important than anything else, the seminaries have to prepare their students for spiritual leadership. For there can be no Christian theology apart from Christian living. Knowledge, learning, intellectual power, do not in themselves make the theologian. Theology comes from the heart as well as the head. And so theological seminaries must be centers of spiritual power. They must be concerned that candidates for the ministry shall be carefully chosen; that they shall acquire habits of prayer and a disciplined Christian life; that they be prepared in every way to be 'messengers, watchmen, and stewards of the Lord.'

All this the Church expects of its seminaries. And now we are prepared to answer the question which is the title of this short outline. It is this—if we desire the present effectiveness of the Church or its future welfare, there is nothing more important than good theological seminaries. But this raises another grave question—is the Church today meeting its responsibility, and especially its financial responsibility, toward the support of its theological seminaries?

THE HOLY EUCHARIST SIMPLIFIED

(Also called the Lord's Supper, the Holy Communion, and the Mass)

In Accordance with Ancient Tradition on the Basis of the Book of Common Prayer

ALMIGHTY GOD, unto whom all hearts are open, all desires known, and from whom no secrets are hid; Cleanse the thoughts of our hearts by the inspiration of thy Holy Spirit, that we may perfectly love thee, and worthily magnify thy holy Name; through Christ our Lord. *Amen.*

COLLECT OF THE DAY (Book of Common Prayer)
HYMN

INSTRUCTION

LESSON from the Old Testament or New Testament
HYMN

GOSPEL (Book of Common Prayer)

¶*When the Priest says* The Holy Gospel for . . . is written in the . . . chapter of St. . . . *the Congregation shall stand and say* Glory be to thee, O Lord, *and at the end,* Thanks be to Thee, O Christ. *Either before or after the Gospel may come Notices and an Instruction or Sermon.*

OFFERING & INTERCESSION

HYMN

¶*The alms shall here be collected and placed upon the altar.*

¶*Then representatives of the congregation shall bring the bread and wine for the Holy Sacrifice, which the Priest shall reverently place upon the altar while all stand. The deacon or server shall stand at the altar.*

¶*Then shall follow the Intercessions which may include:* The Parish and Diocese, The whole Catholic Church, The Faithful departed, The President and all in civil authority, The Family of nations, For Christian education, For Social justice, For the Spread of Christ's Kingdom.

¶*At the end of the Intercessions all shall stand.*

CONSECRATION & COMMUNION

LIFT up your hearts.

We lift them up unto the Lord.

Let us give thanks unto our Lord God.

It is meet and right so to do.

It is very meet, right, and our bounden duty, that we should at all times, and in all places, give thanks unto thee, O Lord, Holy Father, Almighty, Everlasting God.

¶*Here will come the Proper Preface.*

THEREFORE with Angels and Archangels, and with all the company of heaven, we laud and magnify thy glorious Name; evermore praising thee, and saying,

HOLY, HOLY, HOLY, Lord God of hosts, Heaven and earth are full of thy glory: Glory be to thee, O Lord Most High. Amen.

¶*All kneeling.*

ALL glory be to thee, Almighty God, our heavenly Father, for that thou didst give thine only Son Jesus Christ to suffer death upon the Cross for our redemption; who made there a full, perfect, and sufficient sacrifice for the sins of the whole world; and did institute, and command us to continue, a perpetual memory of that his death and sacrifice, until his coming again: For in the night in which he was betrayed, he took Bread; and when he had given thanks, he brake it, and gave it to his disciples, saying, Take, eat, this is my Body, which is given for you; Do this in remembrance of me. Likewise after supper, he took the Cup; and when he had given thanks, he gave it to them, saying, Drink ye all of this; for this is my Blood of the New Covenant, which is shed for you, and for many, for the remission of sins; Do this, as oft as ye shall drink it, in remembrance of me.

WHEREFORE we do celebrate here before thy Divine Majesty, with these thy holy gifts, which we now offer unto thee, the memorial thy Son hath commanded us to make; having in remembrance not only his blessed passion and precious death, but also his mighty resurrection and glorious ascension.

VOUCHSAFE, O merciful Father, to bless and sanctify, with thy Word and Holy Spirit, these thy gifts of bread and wine; that we, receiving them, may be partakers of his most blessed Body and Blood.

AND we earnestly desire thee to accept this our sacrifice of praise and thanksgiving, which we here offer and present, together with ourselves, our souls and bodies, to be a reasonable, holy, and living sacrifice unto thee; beseeching thee that we may all be made one body with thy Son Jesus Christ. And although we are unworthy to offer unto thee any sacrifice; yet we beseech thee to accept this our bounden duty and service; through Jesus Christ our Lord; by whom, and with whom, in the unity of the Holy Ghost, all honour and glory be unto thee, O Father Almighty, world without end. *Amen.*

And now, as our Saviour Christ hath taught us, we have confidence to say,

OUR FATHER, *Who art in heaven, Hallowed be thy Name. Thy kingdom come. Thy will be done. On earth as it is in heaven. Give us this day our daily bread. And forgive us our trespasses, As we forgive those who trespass against us. And lead us not into temptation, But deliver us from evil. For thine is the kingdom, and the power, and the glory, for ever and ever. Amen.*

¶*After a pause, the* Prayer of Humble Access, *as follows:*

WE *do not presume to come to this thy Table, O merciful Lord, trusting in our own righteousness, but in thy manifold and great mercies. We are not worthy so much as to gather up the crumbs under thy Table. But thou art the same Lord, whose property is always to have mercy: Grant us therefore, gracious Lord, so to eat the flesh of thy dear Son Jesus Christ, and to drink his blood, that our sinful bodies may be made clean by his body, and our souls washed through his most precious blood, and that we may evermore dwell in him, and he in us. Amen.*

¶*When the Priest administers the Holy Communion he shall say to each communicant or to all together:* The Body (and Blood) of our Lord Jesus Christ. *And each communicant shall answer:* Amen.

THANKSGIVING

THE Lord be with you.
And with thy spirit.
Let us pray.

ALMIGHTY and everlasting God, we most heartily thank thee, for that thou dost vouchsafe to feed us who have duly received these holy mysteries, with the spiritual food of the most precious Body and Blood of thy Son our Saviour Jesus Christ; and dost assure us thereby of thy favour and goodness towards us; and that we are very members incorporate in the mystical body of thy Son, which is the blessed company of all faithful people; and are also heirs through hope of thy everlasting kingdom, by the merits of his most precious death and passion. And we humbly beseech thee, O heavenly Father, so to assist us with thy grace, that we may continue in that holy fellowship, and do all such good works as thou hast prepared for us to walk in; through Jesus Christ our Lord, to whom, with thee and the Holy Ghost, be all honour and glory, world without end. Amen.

HYMN OR *GLORIA PATRI*

BLESSING

¶*In place of the Blessing from the Book of Common Prayer this old (c.* 200 *A.D.) form of dismissal may be used:* 'And now let each one hasten to do good works, to please God and live aright, devoting himself to the Church, practising the things he has learned, advancing in the service of God.'

NOTES FOR THE CLERGY

THERE is general approval today of the simplification of the Bible, Church doctrine, Church music, and such Prayer Book services as Morning Prayer, to adapt them to young people or to special occasions. It would seem reasonable and not contrary to the mind of the Church to make a similar simplification and adaptation of the Church's chief act of worship. The idea of an inalterable Eucharist is not in fact the primitive one, and did not finally establish itself until the advent of the printing press and the triumph of 'fundamentalism' in scripture interpretation and doctrinal formulation in the XVI century.

Many will miss familiar parts of the Prayer Book here omitted. They may be reminded that the Prayer Book service in its long history has acquired elements out of many different times, places, and theologies. For example, the Commandments, the Kyrie, the Creed, the Confession, the Gloria in Excelsis are all acquisitions, some of them quite late. The original Eucharist was simple, logical, intelligible, and often very short.

The compiler of this service trusts it has no features which contravene Catholic and orthodox tradition, and he is assured by competent liturgists and theologians that such is the case.

The following suggestions are offered:

1. Those who prefer can insert a sung Kyrie, preferably in Greek, immediately before the Collect of the day.

2. The Gospel should be read (from the pulpit or lectern) with dignified ceremonial. Except for this, the beginning of the service may be very informal (perhaps taken by laymen), the priest going to the altar at the Offering.

3. Any of the hymns may be omitted. Or in their place a psalm appropriate to the season, or one of the familiar canticles of Morning or Evening Prayer, may be sung. Hymns may be divided, one or two verses of the same hymn, e.g. 'O come, O come, Emmanuel' in Advent, and 'The royal Banners' in Passiontide, being sung at each place marked 'Hymn.'

4. The Offering of bread and wine should (in accordance with the best liturgical tradition) be given special dignity.

5. Some may prefer to put Intercessions immediately before the blessing. Thus after the period of eucharistic vision we pray for others before we go out to live the eucharistic life among them. They may be very informal, e.g. 'Let us pray for Bishop Brown' or 'for Mrs. Smith, seriously ill,' summing up after each section with a phrase from the Prayer Book, e.g. from the Prayer for the Church or a Collect, followed by the 'Amen.'

6. The service should begin and end quietly, omitting all 'processionals' and 'recessionals.'

INDEX

CPSIA information can be obtained
at www.ICGtesting.com
Printed in the USA
LVHW081032061218
597372LV00039B/592/P